SCHAUM'S

FRENCH

Other Books in Schaum's Easy Outlines Series include:

Schaum's Easy Outline: College Algebra
Schaum's Easy Outline: Calculus
Schaum's Easy Outline: College Physics
Schaum's Easy Outline: Statistics
Schaum's Easy Outline: Programming with C++
Schaum's Easy Outline: College Chemistry
Schaum's Easy Outline: Spanish
Schaum's Easy Outline: German
Schaum's Easy Outline: Organic Chemistry

SCHAUM'S *Easy* OUTLINES

FRENCH

BASED ON SCHAUM'S *Outline of French Grammar* and *French Vocabulary* BY MARY E. COFFMAN CROCKER

ABRIDGEMENT EDITOR: RUPERT T. PICKENS

SCHAUM'S OUTLINE SERIES
McGRAW-HILL

New York San Francisco Washington, D.C. Auckland Bogotá Caracas Lisbon London Madrid Mexico City Milan Montreal New Delhi San Juan Singapore Sydney Tokyo Toronto

MARY E. COFFMAN CROCKER is currently a French editor and consultant in Toronto, Ontario. She was previously Directrice des Editions, Langues secondes, Centre Educatif et Culturel, Montréal, Québec, and Sponsoring Editor, Foreign Language Department, McGraw-Hill Book Company, New York, New York.

RUPERT T. PICKENS is Professor of French and Chair of the Department of French Language and Literature at the University of Kentucky. He received A.B., M.A., and Ph.D. degrees from the University of North Carolina at Chapel Hill.

8 9 10 11 12 13 14 15 DOC DOC 0 9 8

ISBN 0-07-052715-6

Sponsoring Editor: Barbara Gilson
Production Supervisor: Tina Cameron
Editing Supervisor: Maureen B. Walker

McGraw-Hill

A Division of The McGraw-Hill Companies

Contents

Chapter 1
NOUNS AND ARTICLES

IN THIS CHAPTER:

✔ *Gender*
✔ *Nouns of Agency*
✔ *Plural of Compound Nouns*
✔ *The Definite Article*
✔ *The Indefinite Article*
✔ *The Partitive*
✔ *Possession*

Gender

Gender and the Definite Article

Singular Forms

French nouns, unlike English nouns, have gender. Every noun is either masculine or feminine. Most nouns referring specifically to males (people or animals) are masculine; those referring to females are feminine. For other nouns, gender is usually arbitrary and must be memorized.

1

The definite article (*the*) that accompanies masculine nouns is *le*; the feminine definite article is *la*. Both *le* and *la* elide and become *l'* before a vowel or before the letter *h* (mute *h*) in many words: **le garçon** (*the boy*), **le chien** (*the dog*), **le salon** (*the living room*), **l'ami** (*the friend*); **la fille** (*the girl*), **la chienne** (*the dog*), **la chambre** (*the bedroom*), **l'amie** (*the friend*).

The definite article does not elide before *h* (aspirate *h*) in some words: **le homard** (*the lobster*), **la hache** (*the axe*).

Regular Plurals

Most nouns are made plural by adding *-s* to the singular forms; *s* is the most common plural ending. The definite article accompanying all plural nouns, masculine and feminine, is *les*: **le garçon, les garçons, l'ami, les amis, le homard, les homards; la fille, les filles, l'amie, les amies, la hache, les haches.**

Nouns ending in *-s*, *-x*, or *-z* in the singular have no plural ending: **le bras** (*arm*), **les bras**; **la voix** (*voice*), **les voix**; **le nez** (*nose*), **les nez**.

Nouns ending in *-au*, *-eau*, *-eu*, and *-œu* add *-x* to form the plural: **le noyau** (*kernel, pit* [*of fruit*]), **les noyaux**; **le château** (*castle*), **les châteaux**; **le feu** (*fire*), **les feux**; exception: **le pneu** (*tire*), **les pneus**.

Many nouns ending in *-ou* add *-x* to form the plural: **le bijou** (*jewel*), **les bijoux**; **le genou** (*knee*), **les genoux**; exceptions: **les clous** (*nails*), **les trous** (*holes*).

Irregular Plurals

Certain nouns have irregular plurals: **l'aïeul** (*ancestor*), **les aïeux**; **le bonhomme** (*old fellow*), **les bonshommes**; **le ciel** (*sky, heaven*) **les cieux**; **le gentilhomme** (*gentleman*), **les gentilshommes**; **l'œil** (*eye*), **les yeux**; **madame** (*Mrs.*), **mesdames**; **mademoiselle** (*Miss*), **mesdemoiselles**; **monsieur** (*Mr., gentleman*), **messieurs**.

Family names do not have a plural form: **les Dupont**.

Most nouns ending in -*al* in the singular change -*al* to -*aux* to form the plural: **le cheval** (*horse*), **les chevaux**; exceptions: **les bals** (*balls, dances*), **les carnavals** (*carnivals*), **les festivals** (*festivals*). Most nouns ending in -*ail* add *s* to form the plural: **le détail, les détails**; exceptions: **le travail** (*work*), **les travaux**; **le vitrail** (*stained-glass window*), **les vitraux**.

Gender Identification of Nouns by Word Ending

Nouns ending in -*aison*, -*ale*, -*ance*, -*ée*, -*ence*, -*ie*, -*ole*, -*sion*, -*té*, -*tion*, -*ude*, and -*ure* are nearly always feminine: **la maison** (*house*), **la cathédrale**, **la connaissance** (*knowledge, acquaintance*), **la soirée** (*evening, evening party*), **la patience**, **la photographie** (*photograph*), **l'école** (*school*), **la version** (*version, translation*), **la portion**, **la beauté** (*beauty*), **la nation**, **la certitude** (*certainty*), **la facture** (*bill, invoce*); exceptions: **le colisée** (*coliseum*), **le lycée** (*high school*), **le musée** (*museum*), **l'incendie** (masc.) (*conflagration*).

Nouns ending in -*acle*, -*asme*, -*é* (except for -*té*—see above), -*eau*, -*isme*, and -*ment* are nearly always masculine: **le spectacle** (*show, performance*), **le sarcasme**, **le marché** (*market*), **le bateau** (*boat*), - **l'égoïsme** (*selfishness*), **l'enseignement** (*teaching, education*); exceptions: **l'eau** (f.) (*water*), **la jument** (*mare*).

Homographs with Different Meanings
in Masculine and Feminine Forms

l'aide (m.) (*helper*), **l'aide** (f.) (*help*); **le critique** (*critic*), **la critique** (*criticism*); **le guide** (*guide*), **la guide** (*reins*); **le livre** (*book*), **la livre** (*pound*); **le manche** (*handle*), **la manche** (*sleeve*); **le mode** (*method*), **la mode** (*fashion*); **l'office** (m.) (*office, duty*), **l'office** (f.) (*pantry*); **le pendule** (*pendulum*), **la pendule** (*clock*); **le poêle** (*wood stove*), **la poêle** (*frying pan*); **le poste** (*job*), **la poste** (*post office, mail*); **le somme** (*nap*), **la somme** (*sum*); **le tour** (*tour, turn*), **la tour** (*tower*); **le vase** (*vase*), **la vase** (*mud*); **le voile** (*veil*), **la voile** (*sail*).

Nouns of Agency

Nouns of agency are formed on verb stems and represent a person or a thing that performs the action indicated by the verb.

Many agent nouns are formed by adding the endings *-eur* (masculine), *-euse* (feminine) to the present stem (*See* Chap. 5): **le dormeur** (*sleeper*), **la dormeuse**; **le joueur** (*player*), **la joueuse**; **le serveur** (*server*), **la serveuse**; **le vendeur** (*salesperson*), **la vendeuse**.

A few agent nouns derive from the present participle (*See* Chap. 5): **le gagnant** (*winner*), **la gagnante**; **le perdant** (*loser*), **la perdante**; **le servant, la servante**; **le résident, la résidente**.

Many others agent nouns are, historically, based on past participles; these end in a vowel plus *–teur* or *cteur* (m.) and *-trice* or *-ctrice:* **le conservateur, la conservatrice**; **l'acteur, l'actrice**; **le lecteur** (*reader*), **la lectrice**; **le protecteur, la protectrice**; **le persécuteur, la persécutrice.**

Occupations and Trade

Agents

Many nouns denoting occupations and trades are agent nouns. In addition to nouns listed above, examples include: **le chanteur** (*singer*), **la chanteuse**; **le danseur, la danseuse**; **le directeur** (*principal, head, director*) **la directrice**; **le président, la présidente.**

Others

Many other nouns denoting occupations and trades are formed by adding endings such as *-aire* (masculine, feminine); *-ien, -ienne*; *-iste* (masculine, feminine); and *-er, -ère* to roots suggesting lines of work or places of work: **le bibliothécaire** (*librarian*), **la bibliothécaire**; **le mécanicien** (*mechanic*), **la mécanicienne**; **le garagiste** (*garage owner*), **la garagiste**; **le boulanger** (*[bread] baker*), **la boulangère.**

Questions of Gender

Several nouns denoting professions dominated by men until recently do not have feminine forms in standard French: **l'auteur** (*author*), **le chef**

(*chef*), l'**écrivain** (*writer*), l'**ingénieur** (*engineer*), le **médecin** (*physician*), le **ministre** (*[government] minister*), le **peintre** (*painter*), le **professeur** (*professor*).

Conventionally, in order to stress the fact that the professional is a woman, French adds the word *femme*: **une femme écrivain, une femme professeur.** Recent attempts to create new feminine forms for such nouns—for example, *la chéfesse, l'écrivaine, la professeuse*—have been slow to gain acceptance. An exception is the new form l'**avocate** (*lawyer*), derived from the masculine l'**avocat.**

✴ Note!

In conservative, highly formal usage, wives of men occupying certain positions assume their husbands' titles: **madame la présidente/la générale/la directrice**

Plural of Compound Nouns

When a compound noun is formed with two nouns, with a noun and an adjective, or with two adjectives, the plural ending -*s* or -*x* (see above) is added to both elements: **les choux-fleurs** (*cauliflowers*), **les wagons-restaurants** (*dining cars*), **les beaux-frères** (*brothers-in-law, stepbrothers*), **les grands-mères** (*grandmothers*); exceptions: **les timbres-poste** (*postage stamps*), **les pique-niques** (*picnics*).

When a compound noun is formed with a noun and its complement, usually a prepositional phrase, a plural ending is added only to the first element, the noun: **les arcs-en-ciel** (*rainbows*), **les chefs-d'œuvre** (*masterpieces*), **les culs-de-sac** (*dead-end streets*).

When a compound noun is formed with an invariable, usually an adverb or a preposition, followed by a noun, the plural ending is added only to the noun: **les avant-coureurs** (*forerunners*), **les bien-pensants** (*right-thinkers*).

When a compound noun is formed with a verb and its complement, usually neither element takes a plural ending: l'**/les abat-jour** (*lampshade*), **le/les porte-monnaie** (*change purses*); exceptions: **les**

cure-dents (*toothpicks*), **les tire-bouchons** (*corkscrews*), **les couvre-lits** (*bedspreads*).

Other compound nouns that have the same form in the singular and the plural: **l'/les après-midi** (*afternoons*), **le/les hors-d'œuvre** (*canapés*), **le/les tête-à-tête** (*private talks*).

The Definite Article

Special Uses of the Definite Article

With General or Abstract Nouns

Contrary to English usage, in French the definite article must be used with all abstract nouns and with concrete nouns used in a general sense: **L'humanité lutte contre le mal.** (*Humanity fights against evil.*) **Il aime les bananes.** (*He loves bananas.*)

With Professional Titles

When talking about someone who has a professional title, the definite article accompanies the title. Notice that the title is not capitalized: **Le docteur Martin est dentiste.** (*Dr. Martin is a dentist.*)

The article is omitted in direct address: **Au revoir, professeur Bouvert.** (*Goodbye, Professor Bouvert.*)

In formal address, in speaking and in writing, the article is used before professional titles in combination with the courtesy titles *monsieur, madame, mademoiselle*: **madame le professeur Leroy** (*Professor Leroy*), **monsieur le président** (*Mr. President*),

The definite article is never used before courtesy titles (but note that *le monsieur* means *the gentleman*): **Madame Colbert ne vient pas.** (*Mrs. Colbert is not coming.*) **Bonjour, monsieur.** (*Hello, sir.*)

With the Names of Languages and Academic Fields of Study

The definite article is used at all times <u>except</u> when the noun follows *de* or *en* and, in the case of languages, when the noun <u>immediately</u> follows the verb *parler* (*to speak*): **J'étudie la biologie et l'anglais.** (*I'm studying Spanish and English.*) **Il parle très mal le russe.** (*He speaks*

Russian very badly.) **Je ne parle pas japonais.** (*I don't speak Japanese.*) **Elle se spécialise en maths.** (*She majors in mathematics.*) **C'est mon livre d'histoire.** (*That's my history book.*)

With Dates

The definite article precedes the date: **Les cours recommencent le 15 septembre.** (*Courses resume September 15.*) **Je suis né le 20 février 1957.** (*I was born February 20, 1957.*)

With Days of the Week

The definite article is used with a day of the week in the singular to indicate habitual occurrence: **Il enseigne le lundi.** (*He teaches Mondays [every Monday]*).

To emphasize the habitual nature of an action, the plural is used with the plural adjective *tous* (*all*): **Tous les samedis nous allons à la plage.** (*Every Saturday we go to the beach.*)

When a date is accompanied by a day of the week, the article precedes the latter: **Le mariage aura lieu le samedi 20 avril.** (*The wedding will take place Saturday, April 20.*)

With Seasons

The definite article is used with names of the seasons except, for names beginning in a vowel or mute *h*, after *de* and *en*: **Le printemps/ L'été/L'automne/L'hiver est la plus belle saison.** (*Spring/Summer/ Fall/Winter is the most beautiful season.*) **Je vais au bord de la mer en été.** (*I go to the seashore in summer.*) **Je ne travaille pas pendant les vacances d'hiver.** (*I don't work during winter vacation.*) But: **Les fleurs du printemps sont les plus jolies.** (*Spring flowers are the prettiest.*) **Au printemps il fait bon.** (*In spring the weather is nice.*)

With the Names of Continents, Countries, Provinces, American States, Regions, Islands, Mountains, and Rivers

The definite article is used with geographical names except after certain prepositions (*See* Chap. 3): **L'Amérique du Nord est un vaste continent.** (*North America is a vast continent.*) **La France n'est pas**

un très grand pays. (*France is not a very large country.*) **Le Québec est une grande province.** (*Quebec is a large province.*) **Le Madagascar est une île près de l'Afrique.** (*Madagascar is an island near Africa.*) **Les Pyrénées séparent la France et l'Espagne.** (*The Pyrenees separate France and Spain.*) **La Seine est un grand fleuve.** (*The Seine is a great river.*)

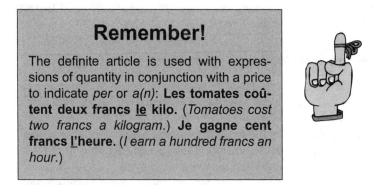

Remember!

The definite article is used with expressions of quantity in conjunction with a price to indicate *per* or *a(n)*: **Les tomates coûtent deux francs le kilo.** (*Tomatoes cost two francs a kilogram.*) **Je gagne cent francs l'heure.** (*I earn a hundred francs an hour.*)

With Parts of the Body and Parts of Articles of Clothing

Very often the definite article is used instead of a possessive adjective with words for parts of the body and parts of clothing; when the noun is the direct object of a verb, possession is shown with an indirect object form of a reflexive or personal pronoun (*See* Chap. 8): **Il se lave les mains.** (*He's washing his hands.*) **Elle me lave les cheveux.** (*She's washing my hair.*) **J'ai le mot au bout de la langue.** (*I have the word on the tip of my tongue.*) **Il s'en va les mains dans les poches.** (*He goes away with his hands in his pockets.*)

Omission of the Definite Article

Before Nouns in Apposition

The definite article is generally not used before a noun in apposition with another noun: **Paris, capital de la France, est une grande ville.** (*Paris, the capital of France, is a large city.*)

After *avec* and *sans* Used with an Abstract Noun

In French, abstract nouns usually occur with the definite article, but not after the prepositions *avec* (*with*) and *sans* (*without*): **Il chante avec passion/sans passion.** (*He sings with/without passion.*)

After *de* Linking Two Nouns

When the preposition *de* introduces a noun as a modifier of another noun, the definite article is not used before the modifier: **La soie est très légère.** (*Silk is very light.*) But: **Elle porte une robe de soie.** (*She is wearing a silk dress.*) **Voilà mon livre d'histoire.** (*There's my history book.*)

Contractions of the Definite Article

à Forms of the definite article contract with the preposition *à* (*at, to*):

　　à + le > au　　　　　　　　**à + les > aux**

The forms *la* and *l'* do not contract: **Je vais au musée.** (*I'm going to the museum.*) **Je parle aux garçons.** (*I'm talking to the boys.*) **Je parle aux jeunes filles.** (*I'm talking to the girls.*) But: **Je vais à la pharmacie.** (*I'm going to the drug store.*) **Je dois aller à l'hôpital.** (*I must go to the hospital.*)

de Forms of the definite article contract with the preposition *de* (*of, from, about*):

　　de + le > du　　　　　　　　**de + les > des**

The forms *la* and *l'* do not contract. **Je parle du garçon.** (*I'm talking about the boy.*) **Je parle des jeunes filles.** (*I'm talking about the girls.*) But: **Je parle de la jeune fille.** (*I'm talking about the girl.*) **Je parle de l'étudiant.** (*I'm talking about the student.*)

The Indefinite Article

The indefinite article in French has singular and plural forms. In the singular (for *a, an*): **un** (m.), **une** (f.); in the plural (for *some, any*): **des** (m. and f.): **un garçon** (*a boy*), **un homme** (*a man*), **des garçons** (*boys, some boys*), **des hommes** (*men, some men*); **une fille** (*a girl*), **une amie** (*a female friend*), **des** filles (*girls, some girls; daughters, some daughters*), **des** amies (*female friends, some friends*).

> Some nouns have two genders: **un** élève, **une** élève (*a pupil*); **un** artiste, **une** artiste (*an artist*); **un** enfant, **une** enfant (*a child*).

When a noun is the direct object of a verb in the negative, or when it follows a negative particle (*See* Chap. 7), the indefinite article is *de* (*d'* before a vowel or mute *h*) for both genders, singular and plural: **Je n'ai pas de voiture.** (*I don't have a car.*) **Il n'a pas d'amies.** (*He has no girl friends.*)

In careful speech and in written French, when an adjective precedes a noun in the plural, the form of the indefinite article is *de* (*d'* before a vowel or mute *h*): **J'ai de bons livres.** (*I have some good books.*) **Il a d'excellents amis.** (*He has excellent friends.*)

Many French speakers say, although they should not write, "J'ai des bons livres." Sometimes, however, when the adjective is considered to be an integral part of the idea, the form *des* is correctly used: **des jeunes filles** (*girls*), **des jeunes gens** (*young people*), **des petits pains** (*rolls*), **des petits pois** (*peas*).

Omission of the Indefinite Article

After the Verb *être*

Contrary to English usage, in French the indefinite article is omitted after *être* (*to be*) when the verb is followed by a noun indicating the subject's nationality, profession, religion, political party, or other affiliation. Notice that in French the words denoting nationality do not begin with a capital letter unless preceded by an article; words denoting religious or other affiliation are never capitalized: **Elle est médecin.** (*She's a doctor.*) **Il est catholique.** (*He's a Catholic.*) **Georges est socialiste.** (*Georges is a socialist.*) **Il est italien.** (*He is an Italian.*)

However, when the noun is modified by an adjective or an adjective clause, the indefinite article is used: **Elle est une catholique dévouée.**

(*She is a devout Catholic.*) **Victor Hugo est <u>un</u> auteur <u>que tout le monde connaît</u>.** (*Victor Hugo is an author everyone knows.*) When *c'est* means *he is* or *she is* or *ce sont* means *they are*, the indefinite articles is used: **<u>C'est</u> <u>un</u> avocat.** (*He is <u>a</u> lawyer.*) **<u>Ce</u> sont <u>des</u> Américains.** (*They are Americans.*) After *être* in the negative the indefinite article is *un, une,* or *des* and does not become *de*: **Ce n'est pas <u>un</u> avocat.** (*He is not a lawyer.*) **Ce ne sont pas <u>des</u> Américains.** (*They are not Americans.*)

The Partitive

In French, mass nouns—words that name things that cannot be counted, such as *milk, sugar, coffee, oil, gasoline*—are always accompanied by a partitive article. In English the partitive is represented by *any* or *some* or by nothing at all. The partitive exists only in the singular: **du** (m.), **de la** (f.), **de l'** (m. and f., before a vowel or mute *h*): **J'ai <u>de la</u> soupe.** (*I have some soup.*) **Voudrais-tu <u>du</u> café?** (*Would you like any coffee?*) **Il a encore <u>de l'</u>essence.** (*He still has gas.*) **Il prend son café avec <u>du</u> lait.** (*He takes his coffee with milk.*)

When a noun is the direct object of a verb in the negative, or when it follows a negative particle (*See* Chap. 7), the partitive is **de** (**d'** before a vowel or mute *h*): **Je n'ai plus <u>de</u> soupe.** (*I don't have any more soup.*) **Non, merci, pas <u>de</u> café pour moi.** (*No, thanks, no coffee for me.*) **Il n'a pas <u>d'</u>essence.** (*He doesn't have any gasoline.*)

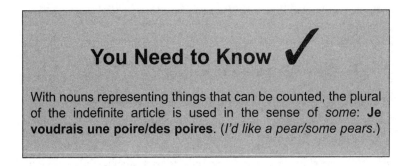

You Need to Know ✓

With nouns representing things that can be counted, the plural of the indefinite article is used in the sense of *some*: **Je voudrais une poire/des poires.** (*I'd like a pear/some pears.*)

Omission of the Partitive

After *sans*

The partitive is not used after the preposition *sans* (*without*): **Il est sans argent.** (*He is without money.*)

In the Construction *ni . . . ni*

The partitive does not occur in the negative construction *ni . . . ni* (*neither . . . nor*) (*See* Chap. 7).: **Il n'a ni pain ni argent.** (*He has neither bread nor money.*)

The Partitive Versus the Definite and Indefinite Articles

The definite article is used with nouns in a general sense; the partitive is used with an undetermined quantity of an item that cannot be counted: **Il aime le café.** (*He likes coffee*—that is, all coffee in general.) **Il boit du café.** (*He's drinking coffee*—that is, some of all the coffee there is).

Some nouns can represent things that both can and cannot be counted: **J'aime le gâteau.** (*I like cake*—that is, all cake in general.) **Voici le gâteau que j'ai fait.** (*Here's the cake I made*—that is, a particular cake). **Voici un gâteau.** (*Here's a cake.*) **Voici des gâteaux.** (*Here are some cakes.*) **Voici du gâteau.** (*Here's some cake, a piece of cake.*) **Il aime le fromage et il va prendre du fromage.** (*He likes cheese and he is going to eat some cheese.*)

The Partitive after the Preposition *de*

As a general rule, the partitive disappears after the preposition *de*.

Expressions of Quantity

French expressions of quantity generally consist of an adverb or a noun phrase. When a noun accompanies an expression of quantity, it is introduced by the preposition *de* (*d'* before a vowel or mute *h*). Examples include **assez** (*enough*), **autant** (*as much*), **beaucoup** (*much, a lot*), **moins** (*less*), **peu** (*little*), **plus** (*more*), **trop** (*too much*), **tant** (*so much*), **un peu** (*a little*), **une boîte** (*a box*), **une bouteille** (*a bottle*), **une douzaine** (*a dozen*), **un kilo** (*a kilogram*), **un litre** (*a liter*), **une livre** (*a pound*), **une tasse** (*a cup*), **une tranche** (*a slice*), **un verre** (*a glass*): **Elle veut <u>un peu d'eau</u>.** (*She wants a little water.*) **J'achète <u>une livre de</u> beurre.** (*I'm buying a pound of butter.*)

A few expressions of quantity require the definite article: <u>**la plupart de la**</u> classe (*most of the class*), <u>**bien des**</u> fois (*many times*). The adjectives *plusieurs* (*several*) and *quelques* (*some, a few*) are not followed by *de*: **Il a plusieurs amies.** (*He has several girl friends.*) **J'ai quelques sous dans la poche.** (*I have a few pennies in my pocket.*)

Other Expressions

Nouns accompanying certain idiomatic expressions are introduced by *de* (*d'* before a vowel or mute *h*): *avoir besoin de* (*to need*), *avoir envie de* (*to want*), etc.: **J'ai envie de fraises.** (*I want strawberries.*)

Possession

In French, possession is shown by use of the preposition *de* (*of*). The noun representing the person or object being possessed is most often accompanied by an article, while the possessor is always introduced by *de* (*d'* before a vowel or mute *h*): **Voilà <u>la</u> voiture <u>de</u> mon père.** (*There's my father's car.*) **J'ai <u>les</u> livres <u>d'</u>André.** (*I have André's books.*) **La fille <u>du</u> professeur arrive.** (*The professor's daughter is arriving.*) **C'est <u>le</u> chien <u>d'un</u> bon maître.** (*He is the dog of a good master.*)

In one construction involving the verb *être* (*to be*), however, the noun representing the possessor is introduced by *à*: **Cette radio est <u>à</u> moi.** (*This radio is mine.*) **Ce livre est <u>au</u> professeur.** (*This book is the professor's.*)

Chapter 2
ADJECTIVES
AND ADVERBS

Adjectives

Gender and Number

Variable adjectives must agree in gender and number with the nouns they modify. The masculine singular is considered the basic form of the adjective; endings are added to it to make the adjective feminine and plural. Most French adjectives are variable; however, some are invariable—they exist in only one form regardless of gender and number.

Variable Adjectives:
Formation of Feminine Adjectives

Regular Forms

Most adjectives add -*e* to the masculine singular form to make it feminine. In speaking, the ending -*e* is not articulated, but it indicates that a final consonant, generally silent in the masculine singular, is pronounced: **grand** (masculine), **grande** (feminine) (*big, tall*).

A few common regular adjectives follow (note that proper adjectives are not capitalized): **américain, américaine** (*American*); **amusant, amusante** (*amusing*); **chaud, chaude** (*hot*); **court, courte** (*short*); **droit, droite** (*straight*); **gris, grise** (*gray*).

Adjectives ending in a vowel or a pronounced consonant have the same pronunciation in the masculine and feminine: **bleu, bleue** (*blue*); **joli, jolie** (*pretty*); **égal, égale** (*equal*); **sûr, sûre** (*sure*).

Some adjectives end in -*e* in the masculine singular form; neither spelling nor pronunciation changes in the feminine singular: **agréable** (*pleasant*), **difficile** (*difficult*), **gauche** (*left, left-hand*), **jaune** (*yellow*), **large** (*wide*), **malade** (*sick*), **pauvre** (*poor*), **rapide** (*fast*), **sale** (*dirty*).

Adjectives Ending in -*el, -eil, -en, -on, -et* and –*s*

Adjectives ending, in the masculine singular, in –*el, -eil, -en, -on, -et*, and some ending in –*s*, double the final consonant before adding -*e* to form the feminine singular: **ancien, ancienne** (*old, ancient*); **bas, basse** (*low*); **bon, bonne** (*good*); **cruel, cruelle** (*cruel*); **muet, muette** (*mute*); **pareil, pareille** (*similar*); **parisien, parisienne** (*Parisian*).

Adjectives Ending in -*er*

Adjectives ending, in the masculine singular, in -*er* form the feminine by adding -*e* and by adding the *accent grave* (note that the final -*r* is pronounced in one-syllable masculine forms): **amer, amère** (*bitter*); **cher, chère** (*dear, expensive*); **étranger, étrangère** (*foreign*).

Adjectives Ending in –*x*

Adjectives ending in -*x* in the masculine singular form the feminine singular by changing -*x* to –*se*: **amoureux, amoureuse** (*in love*); **heureux, heureuse** (*happy*); **jaloux, jalouse** (*jealous*); exceptions: **doux, douce** (*sweet*); **faux, fausse** (*false*); **roux, rousse** (*red-headed*).

Adjectives Ending in -*eur*

Many adjectives in this class are identical with nouns of agency (*See* Chap. 1). The feminine forms depend on whether the ending is added directly to a verb stem (masculine -*eur*, feminine -*euse*) or consists of a vowel or a *c* plus –*teur* (masculine), (feminine –*trice*): **menteur, menteuse** (*lying*); **trompeur, trompeuse** (*deceitful*); **conservateur, conservatrice** (*conservative*); **créateur, créatrice** (*creative*).

Other adjectives ending in -*eur* are not concerned with agency; formation of the feminine is regular: **antérieur, antérieure** (*anterior*); **extérieur, extérieure** (*exterior*); **meilleur, meilleure** (*better, best*).

Adjectives Ending in -*f*

Adjectives ending in -*f* in the masculine singular form the feminine by changing -*f* to –*ve* (note the accent mark in *brève*): **bref, brève** (*brief*); **neuf, neuve** (*new, brand new*); **sportif, sportive** (*athletic*).

Adjectives Ending in -*c*

Adjectives ending in -*c* in the masculine singular regularly form the feminine by changing -*c* to -*che* (only the -*c* in *sec* is pronounced; notice the accent mark in *sèche*): **blanc, blanche** (*white*); **franc, franche** (*frank*); **sec, sèche** (*dry*).

CHAPTER 2: Adjectives and Adverbs 17

> ## ✳ Important Point!
>
> ### Irregular Adjectives
>
> Some adjectives have feminine forms that are irregular either phonetically or orthographically (in *gentil* the *-l* is not pronounced): **aigu, aiguë** (*sharp*); **ambigu, ambiguë** (*ambiguous*); **favori, favorite** (*favorite*); **frais, fraîche** (*fresh, cool*); **gentil, gentille** (*kind, nice*); **long, longue** (*long*); **malin, maligne** (*clever, sly*).

Adjectives with Special Forms in the Masculine Singular

Five adjectives have special forms in the masculine singular that are used before nouns beginning in a vowel or mute *h*: **beau, bel** (m.), **belle** (f.) (*beautiful*); **fou, fol** (m.), **folle** (f.) (*foolish*); **mou, mol** (m.), **molle** (f.) (*soft*); **nouveau, nouvel** (m.), **nouvelle** (f.) (*new*); **vieux, vieil** (m.), **vieille** (f.) (*old*): **C'est un beau garçon.** (*He's a handsome boy.*) **C'est un bel homme.** (*He's a handsome man.*) **L'homme est beau.** (*The man is handsome.*) **C'est un nouvel hôtel.** (*It's a new hotel.*) **L'hôtel est nouveau.** (*The hotel is new.*)

The Plural of Variable Adjectives

Feminine Plurals

All feminine adjectives are perfectly regular in the formation of the plural by adding *-s* to the feminine singular form: **de grandes villes** (*big cities*), **de belles femmes** (*beautiful women*), **des phrases ambiguës** (*ambiguous sentences*), **des langues menteuses** (*lying tongues*).

Regular Masculine Plurals

The plural of masculine adjectives is usually formed by adding *-s* to the singular form: **de petits garçons** (*little boys*), **de grands hommes** (*big men*), **des boxeurs amateurs** (*amateur boxers*).

The Plural of Adjectives Ending in -*s* and –*x*

Adjectives ending in -*s* or -*x* in the singular have the same form in the plural: **de gros pois** (*fat peas*), **des amis heureux** (*happy friends*).

The Plural of Adjectives Ending in -*eu* and -*eau*

Adjectives ending in -*eu* and -*eau* regularly add -*x* to form the plural: **des mots hébreux** (*Hebrew words*), **de beaux livres** (*beautiful books*); exception: **des yeux bleus** (*blue eyes*).

The Plural of Adjectives Ending in -*ou*

Adjectives ending in -*ou* add -*s* to form the plural: **des oreillers mous** (*soft pillows*), **des programmes fous** (*foolish programs*).

The Plural of Adjectives Ending in -*al*

Adjectives ending in -*al* regularly change -*al* to -*aux* to form the plural: **un château médiéval** (*a medieval castle*), **des châteaux médiévaux**; **un acte illégal** (*an illegal act*), **des actes illégaux**; exceptions: **des contes banals** (*banal stories*), **des moments fatals** (*fateful moments*), **des jugements finals** or **finaux** (*final judgments*); **des pays natals** (*native countries*), **des chantiers navals** (*naval shipyards*).

Invariable Adjectives

A few adjectives and adjective phrases are invariable—that is, they use the same form for singular and plural and masculine and feminine. Such adjectives are often nouns that are used as adjectives: **chic** (*stylish*): **une femme/des hommes/des femmes chic**; **ivoire** (*ivory*): **des papiers/joues ivoire**; **orange** (*orange*): **des cheveux/des blouses orange**; **marron** (*brown*): **un œil/des yeux marron, une robe/des robes marron**; **bon marché** (*cheap*): **un livre/des livres bon marché**.

When nouns denoting the points of the compass are used as adjectives, they are invariable: **la zone nord/est/sud/ouest/sud-est**, etc.

When a variable color adjective is modified by **clair** (*light in color*) or **foncé** (*dark*), the adjective phrase is invariable: **une robe bleu clair** (*a light blue dress*), **des chaussures bleu foncé** (*dark blue shoes*).

Shifts in Gender

Three nouns are masculine in the singular and feminine in the plural: **amour** (*love*), **délice** (*delight*), **orgue** (*organ* [musical instrument]): **un amour fou, des amours folles; un grand délice, de grandes délices; un bel orgue, de belles orgues.**
The plural noun **les gens** (*people*) is masculine; however, an adjective preceding it takes the form of the feminine: **Les gens sont bons.** (*The people are good.*) **Il y a de vieilles gens.** (*There are old people.*)

The Position of Adjectives

The normal position of adjectives is following the noun, particularly those indicating color, shape, nationality, origin, religion, profession, or classification, and past participles used as adjectives: **une robe bleue** (*a blue dress*), **une maison carrée** (*a square house*), **une fille française** (*a French girl*), **une église catholique** (*a Catholic church*), **le parti libéral** (*the liberal party*), **l'art classique** (*classical art*), **la porte ouverte** (*the open door*), **la semaine passée** (*last week*).

Certain adjectives, however, regularly precede the noun: **autre** (*other*): **l'autre livre; bon** (*good*): **un bon vin; beau** (*beautiful, handsome*): **de belles femmes; grand** (*great, big*): **une grande maison; jeune** (*young*): **un jeune enfant; joli** (*pretty*): **la jolie scène; long** (*long*): **une longue histoire; mauvais** (*bad*): **un mauvais garçon; petit** (*small*): **un petit appartement; vieux** (*old*): **un vieil homme.**

A very few adjectives may precede or follow the noun without discernable shifts in meaning: **court** (*short*): **une robe courte, une courte histoire; gros** (*fat*): **une grosse femme, un homme gros; méchant** (*bad, naughty*): **un chien méchant, un méchant chien.**

When adjectives are modified by a long adverb or by an adverb phrase, the adjective phrase normally follows the noun: **une histoire complètement bête** (*an utterly stupid story*), **une maison pas du tout jolie** (*a house not in the least pretty*).

A noun may be modified by a both an adjective preceding it and an adjective following it: **une belle robe bleue** (*a beautiful blue dress*), **les grands boulevards parisiens** (*the grand boulevards of Paris*). A noun may be modified by two adjectives that normally precede; generally, the adjective closer to the noun is considered integral to the noun: **une jolie petite fille** (*a pretty little girl*), **un petit jeune homme** (*a small young man*).

When a noun is modified by two adjectives that normally follow, the adjectives are linked by *et* (*and*): **un garçon intéressant et intelligent** (*an interesting, intelligent boy*).

Adjectives that Change Meaning According to Position

Several adjectives have different meanings depending on whether they precede or follow the noun. Adjectives tend to have their basic, literal meanings when they are in their normal position, either preceding or following the noun; out of their normal position, they take on figurative meanings: **ancien** (*old, ancient*): **l'histoire ancienne** (*ancient history*), **l'ancien président** (*the former president*); **brave** (*brave*): **un homme brave** (*a brave man*), **un brave homme** (*a good fellow*); **certain** (*certain, sure*): **un risque certain** (*a sure risk*), **un certain sourire** (*a certain smile*), **un certain monsieur** (*a certain gentleman*); **cher** (*dear*): **un cher ami** (*a dear friend*), **une robe chère** (*an expensive dress*); **dernier** (*last in place*): **la dernière maison à gauche** (*the last house on the left*), **la semaine dernière** (*last week*); **différent** (*different*): **des expériences différentes** (*different [kinds of] experiences*), **de différentes expériences** (*different [various] experiences*); **grand** (*great, big*): **un grand écrivain** (*a great writer*), **un homme grand** (*a tall man*); **haut** (*high*): **un mur haut** (*a high wall*), **la haute culture** (*high culture*); **honnête** (*honest*): **un homme honnête** (*an honest man*), **un honnête homme** (*a worthy man*); **même** (*same*): **la même chose** (*the same thing*), **la chose même** (*the thing itself*), **ce jour même** (*that very day*); **nouveau** (*new*): **une auto nouvelle** (*a new car*), **une nouvelle auto** (*a different car*); **pauvre** (*poor*): **un homme pauvre** (*a poor man*), **le pauvre homme** (*the unfortunate man*); **prochain** (*next*): **le mariage prochain** (*the next wedding*), **le prochain mariage** (*the upcoming wedding*); **propre** (*clean, proper*): **une maison propre** (*a clean house*), **le mot propre** (*the proper* *word)*, **ta propre** maison (*your own house*), **les propres** mots (*the very words*); **sale** (*dirty*): **une chambre sale** (*a dirty room*), **une sale affaire** (*a disgusting affair*); **seul** (*alone*): **un homme seul** (*a man alone*), **le seul homme** (*the only man*); **vrai** (*true, truthful*): **une histoire vraie** (*a true story*), **le vrai Louis XIV** (*the real Louis XIV*).

Adverbs

Formation of Adverbs Related to Adjectives

Adverbs are regularly formed with the ending *-ment*. Adverbs modify a verb, an adjective, or another adverb; they are invariable.

Regular Forms

Most adverbs are formed by adding *-ment* to the feminine form of an adjective: **finale** > **finalement** (*finally*), **forte** > **fortement** (*strongly*), **naturelle** > **naturellement** (*naturally*); **complète** > **complètement** (*completely*), **sérieuse** > **sérieusement** (*seriously*); **nouvelle** > **nouvellement** (*recently*), **douce** > **doucement** (*softly*).

If the masculine form of the adjective ends in a vowel, *-ment* is added to the masculine form: **hardi** > **hardiment** (*boldly*), **vrai** > **vraiment** (*truly, really*), **décidé** > **décidément** (*decidely*), **absolu** > **absolument** (*absolutely*); exception: **gai** > **gaiement** or **gaîment** (*gaily*).

Some adjectives ending in *-u* add a circumflex accent (^) to the *-u* when forming the adverb (cf. *gaîment*, above): **assidu** > **assidûment** (*assiduously*), **continu** > **continûment** (*continuously*).

In a few adverbs the final mute *-e* of the feminine adjective is changed to *-é* before the ending *–ment*: **aveugle** > **aveuglément** (*blindly*), **commode** > **commodément** (*conveniently*), **précise** > **précisément** (*precisely*), **profonde** > **profondément** (*deeply, profoundly*).

If the an adjective ends in *-ant* or *-ent* in the masculine singular, the adverb is formed by changing *-nt* to *-mment* (in speech, *-amment* and *-emment* sound alike): **abondant** > **abondamment** (*abundantly*), **décent** > **décemment** (*decently*); exceptions: **lent** > **lentement** (*slowly*).

Irregular Adverbs

A few adverbs ending in -*ment* have stems that do not conform with the rules above: **bref, brève > brièvement** (*briefly*); **grave > gravement** or **grièvement** (*gravely*); **gentil, gentille > gentiment** (*nicely*); **impuni, impunie > impunément** (*with impunity*).

Some other adverbs differ altogether from the corresponding adjectives; a few have no corresponding adjectives: **bon > bien** (*well*), **mauvais > mal** (*badly*), **meilleur > mieux** (*better*), **moindre > moins** (*less*), **petit > peu** (*little*); **plus** (*more*), **vite** (*fast*).

In a few cases, often in idiomatic expressions, the masculine singular form of the adjective serves as an adverb: **Il parle bas.** (*He speaks low [softly].*) **Cette robe coûte cher.** (*This dress costs a lot.*) **Elle voit clair.** (*She sees clearly [=she understands].*) **Il s'arrête court.** (*He stops short.*) **Il m'a coupé court.** (*He cut me right off.*) **Ils travaillent dur.** (*They work hard.*) **Il crie fort.** (*He's screaming loudly.*) **Il parle haut.** (*He is speaking loudly.*) **Je l'ai cassé net.** (*I broke it clean through.*)

Position of Adverbs

Adverbs modifying a verb follow the verb in simple tenses: **Il parle rapidement.** (*He speaks rapidly.*)

Adverbs modifying the whole sentence may normally come at the beginning, but may also end the sentence: **Heureusement, il l'a bien fait.** (*Fortunately, he did it well.*) **Il l'a bien fait, heureusement.** (*He did it well, fortunately.*)

In compound tenses, short, common adverbs and some adverbs of time and manner are placed between the auxiliary verb and the past participle. Some of these are **assez** (*enough*), **bien** (*well*), **beaucoup** (*very much, a lot*), **bientôt** (*soon*), **déjà** (*already*), **encore** (*still*), **enfin** (*finally*), **jamais** (*never*), **mal** (*badly*), **mieux** (*better*), **moins** (*less*), **souvent** (*often*), **toujours** (*always, still*), **trop** (*too much*), and **vite** (*fast*): **Elle a beaucoup parlé.** (*She talked a lot.*) **Nous avons bien dormi.** (*We slept well.*) **Elle est vite descendue.** (*She came down quickly.*)

Adverbs of place, adverbs ending in -ment, and certain adverbs of time, such as **aujourd'hui** (*today*), **hier** (*yesterday*), **avant-hier** (*the day before yesterday*), and **tard** (*late*), usually follow the past participle, although sometimes they may come at the beginning of the sentence: **Elle est arrivée hier.** (*She arrived yesterday.*) **Ils ont voyagé partout.** (*They traveled everywhere.*) **Elle a compris facilement.** (*She easily understood.*)

An adverb modifying an infinitive may precede or follow it: **Je voudrais toujours garder mon sang-froid/Je voudrais garder toujours mon sang-froid.** (*I would always like to keep my cool.*)

Comparison of Adjectives and Adverbs

Regular Comparisons

The comparative is formed by placing **plus** (*more*), **moins** (*less*), **aussi** (*as*), or **si** (*so*) before and **que** (*than, as*)—**qu'** before a vowel or mute *h*—after the adjective or adverb. Remember that the adjective, unless it is invariable, agrees in number and gender with the noun or pronoun it modifies; adverbs are invariable.

1. Comparisons of superiority: **plus ... que** (*more ... than*): **Cette robe est plus belle que l'autre.** (*This dress is more beautiful than the other one.*) **Il parle plus vite que moi.** (*He speaks faster than I.*)

2. Comparisons of equality: **aussi ... que** (*as ... as*): **Elle est aussi forte que lui.** (*She is as strong as he.*) **Charles parle aussi couramment que Pierre.** (*Charles speaks as fluently as Pierre.*)

3. Comparisons of inferiority: **moins ... que** (*less ... than*): **Cette robe est moins chère que l'autre.** (*This dress is less expensive than the other one.*) **Ce garçon parle moins poliment que l'autre.** (*This boy speaks less politely than the other one.*)

In negative sentences *aussi* becomes *si*, especially in careful speech and in written French: **Elle ne parle pas si vite que son frère.** (*She does not speak so rapidly as her brother.*)

Plus and *moins* also function as adverbs of quantity in sentences that are not comparisons; like nearly all expressions of quantity, they take *de* (rather than *que*) before the noun phrase: **Je travaille plus de soixante heures par semaine.** (*I work more than sixty hours a week.*) **Il y a moins de vingt personnes inscrites au cours.** (*There are fewer* *than* twenty people registered for the course.) But in comparisons: **Je travaille plus que vous.** (*I work more than you.*) **Il y en a moins qu'auparavant.** (*There are fewer than before.*)

Plus de and moins de, as adverbs of quantity, along with *autant de* (*as much as*), may also occur in comparisons: **J'ai plus de livres que lui.** (*I have more books than he.*) **J'ai autant de clients que jamais.** (*I have as many clients as ever.*)

When a noun clause depends upon a comparative, expletive *ne* (*n'* before a vowel or mute *h*) is used in the clause in careful speech and in written French (expletive *ne* does not negate the verb): **Il est plus intelligent que vous ne le pensez.** (*He is more intelligent than you think.*) **Elle est plus intelligente qu'elle n'en a l'air.** (*She is more intelligent than she appears.*)

Irregular Comparatives

A very few common adjectives and adverbs have irregular forms for the comparative of superiority. The comparative forms of adjectives agree in gender and number with the nouns they modify; adverbs are invariable: **bon** (*good*) > **meilleur**; **mauvais** (*bad*) > **plus mauvais** as well as **pire** (rare); **petit** (*small*) > **plus petit** as well as **moindre** (very rare); **bien** (*well*) > **mieux**; **mal** (*badly*) > **plus mal** as well as **pis** (very rare); **peu** (*little*) > **moins**; **beaucoup** (*much, a lot*) > **plus**: **C'est un bon livre; il est meilleur que l'autre.** (*It's a good book; it is better than the other one.*) **Cette pomme est meilleure que l'autre.** (*This apple is better than the other one.*) **Paul parle mieux que Louis.** (*Paul speaks better than Louis.*) **Il travaille moins qu'elle.** (*He works less than she.*) **Cette note est plus mauvaise que l'autre/pire que l'autre.** (*This grade is worse than the other one.*) **Il chante plus mal que Marie/ pis que Marie.** (*He sings badly; he sings worse than Marie.*)

Comparisons of equality and inferiority are formed with the regular form of the adjective or adverb in the positive degree: **Cette note est aussi bonne que l'autre.** (*This grade is as good as the others.*) **Marie chante moins mal que lui.** (*Marie sings less badly than he.*)

The Superlative

The superlative degree of adjectives is formed by adding the definite article *le*, *la*, or *les* to the comparative. The adjective maintains its normal position relative to the noun. The preposition *de* commonly follows the superlative to express *in* or *of*: **Marc est l'étudiant le plus fort de la classe.** (*Marc is the smartest student in the class.*) **C'est la plus belle peinture de toutes.** (*This is the most beautiful painting of all.*) **Ce sont les peintures les moins valables du musée.** (*These are the least valuable paintings in the museum.*) **C'est le pire de tous.** (*He is the worst of all.*) **Ce sont les meilleures pommes de la région.** (*These are the best apples in the region.*)

The superlative degree of adverbs is formed by adding the article *le* to the comparative: **Elle chante le mieux de tous les étudiants.** (*She sings the best of all the students.*) **Il attend le plus patiemment du monde.** (*He waits the most patiently in the world.*)

Le pis does not exist as a superlative adverb, but as a noun: **Le pis de l'affaire c'est qu'il a échoué.** (*The worst of the matter is that he failed.*)

Two adjectives marking the relative ages of siblings—*cadet, cadette* (*younger, youngest*) and *aîné(e)*(*elder, eldest*)—do not have comparative or superlative degrees: **C'est mon frère cadet.** (*He is my younger brother.*) **C'est la cadette.** (*She is the youngest child.*)

You Need to Know ✔

Useful Phrases with Comparatives and Superlatives

1. **plus . . . plus** (*the more . . . the more*), **moins . . . moins** (*the less . . . the less*), **plus . . . moins** (*the more . . . the less*), **moins . . . plus** (*the less . . . the more*): **Plus je lis ce livre, plus je l'aime.** (*The more I read this book, the better I like it.*) **Plus je fais le ménage, moins j'en ai envie.** (*The more I do housework, the less I feel like doing it.*)

2. **de plus en plus** (*more and more*), **de moins en moins** (*less and less*), **de mieux en mieux** (*better and better*), **de mal en pis** (*worse and worse*): **Ce travail devient de plus en plus difficile.** (*This work is getting harder and harder.*) **Elle chante de mieux en mieux.** (*She sings better and better.*) **Les choses vont de mal en pis.** (*Things are getting worse and worse/going from bad to worse.*)

3. **d'autant plus . . que** (*all the more . . . because*): **Il est d'autant plus heureux qu'il a un jardin.** (*He is all the happier because he has a garden.*)

4. **tant mieux** (*so much the better*), **tant pis** (*so much the worse, too bad*): **Il est toujours au bord de la mer? Tant mieux.** (*He's still at the beach? So much the better.*)

es

jectives

Poss.__ jectives identify the possessor(s) of a thing or things and refer to the persons of the verb. In French the possessive adjective, like all adjectives, agrees in gender and number with the noun it modifies, not with those of the possessor(s).

	masculine		feminine	
	singular	plural	singular	plural
my	mon	mes	ma	mes
your (fam.)	ton	tes	ta	tes
his, her, its	son	ses	sa	ses
our	notre	nos	notre	nos
your (pl., formal)	votre	vos	votre	vos
their	leur	leurs	leur	leurs

J'ai <u>mon</u> livre, <u>ma</u> serviette, et <u>mes</u> lunettes. (*I have my book, my briefcase, and my glasses.*) **Elle a <u>son</u> livre, <u>sa</u> serviette, et <u>ses</u> lunettes.** (*She has her book, her briefcase, and her glasses.*)

In the feminine singular, the forms *mon, ton,* and *son* are used before a vowel or mute *h:* **Voilà <u>mon</u> amie Hélène.** (*There's my friend Hélène.*) **C'est <u>son</u> ex-femme.** (*She is his ex-wife.*)

The possessive adjective is repeated before each noun in a series: **Tu dois écrire à <u>ta</u> sœur, à <u>tes</u> parents, et à <u>ton</u> oncle.** (*You must write to your sister, parents, and uncle.*)

Use of the Definite Article as a Possessive

The definite article is used instead of the possessive adjective when referring to parts of the body, to parts of personal clothing, or to mental faculties if the identity of the possessor is clear: **Il a <u>les</u> mains dans <u>les</u> poches.** (*He has his hands in his pockets.*) **Il a baissé <u>la</u> tête.** (*He* *lowered his head.*) **Elle a perdu la mémoire.** (*She lost her memory.*) **Elle a les yeux marron.** (*Her eyes are brown.*)

Often possession of parts of the body or mental faculties is indicated by the use of the indirect object form of personal pronouns before a verb: **Elle m'a tordu le bras.** (*She twisted my arm.*) **Je me suis cassé la jambe.** (*I broke my leg.*) **Cela leur a glacé le sang.** (*That made their blood run cold.*)

However, when the possessor's identity is not clear or when emphasis is desired, the possessive adjective may be used, especially with the verbs *montrer* (*to show*), *regarder* (*to look at*), and *voir* (*to see*): **Ses yeux sont d'un noir profond.** (*Her eyes are deep black.*) **Elle a regardé mes cheveux.** (*She looked at my hair.*)

The Third Singular with *chacun, on, personne,* and *tout le monde*

The possessives *son/sa/ses* are most frequently used in reference to the indefinites *chacun* (*each one*), *on* (*one, people,* "*you*," "*they*"), and *tout le monde* (*everyone*): **Chacun a ses défauts.** (*Each one has his/her faults.*) **On n'est pas méchant par nature.** (*People are not evil by nature.*) **Tout le monde fait de son mieux.** (*Everyone does his best.*)

Demonstrative Adjectives

French has one set of demonstrative adjectives for both *this/these* and *that/those*:

singular: **ce, cet** (m.), **cette** (f.)
plural: **ces** (m. and f.)

In the masculine singular, the form *cet* is used before vowels or mute *h.*: **Ce garçon est beau.** (*That boy is handsome.*) **Cet hôtel a deux étoiles.** (*This hotel has two stars.*) **Cette fille est jolie.** (*This girl is pretty.*) **Ces livres sont intéressants.** (*These books are interesting.*)

When it is necessary to specify location, the invariable adverbs *ci* (*here*) and *là* (*there*) are affixed to the end of the noun with a hyphen: **Je veux ce livre-ci.** (*I want this book.*) **Je prends ces oranges-ci et ces abricots-là.** (*I'll take these oranges and those apricots.*)

Indefinite Adjectives and Adjective Expressions

aucun *Aucun(e)* (*no*) modifies the subject or the complement of a verb, which is preceded by the negative particle *ne* (*n'*): **<u>Aucun</u> travail n'est trop difficile.** (*<u>No</u> work is too hard.*) **Je <u>ne</u> vois <u>aucune</u> peinture qui me plaise.** (*I see <u>no</u> painting I like.*)

certain *Certain(e)* (*certain*) is used before a noun without an article, generally in the plural, as the equivalent of *quelque* (below): **<u>Certaines</u> choses sont difficiles; d'autres ne le sont pas.** (*Certain things are difficult; others are not.*)

chaque *Chaque* (*each, every*) is used before the noun: **Chaque personne a son pays.** (*Each person has his/her own country.*) **Il dit cela chaque fois qu'il fait un discours.** (*He says that every time he gives a speech.*)

différent(es), divers(es) These synonyms occur before a noun without an article in the sense of *various*: **<u>Divers</u> professeurs ont proposé <u>différents</u> projects.** (*<u>Different</u> professors proposed <u>various</u> projects.*)

maint *Maint* is used before a noun without an article in the singular (*many a, various*) or in the plural (*many*): **<u>Maint</u> jeune homme apprend par l'expérience.** (*<u>Many a</u> young man learns from experience.*) **<u>Maintes</u> fois elle a proposé des solutions.** (*<u>Many times</u> she proposed solutions.*)

n'importe This verbal expression combines with the interrogative adjective *quel* to signify *no matter what (which)*: **Téléphonez-moi à <u>n'importe quelle</u> heure.** (*Telephone me at <u>any</u> hour.*) **Ils s'arrêtaient à <u>n'importe quels</u> hôtels.** (*They stopped at <u>no matter what</u> hotels.*)

plusieurs This invariable adjective is used before a noun in the plural, without an article, to signify *several*: **Il a <u>plusieurs</u> belles chemises.** (*He has <u>several</u> beautiful shirts.*)

quelque *Quelque* means *a little, some, some (any) kind of a* in the singular and *some, a few, several* in the plural: **Il me reste <u>quelque</u> temps.** (*I have <u>a little</u> time left.*) **Elle a acheté <u>quelques</u> livres.** (*She bought <u>a few</u> books.*) **Il a <u>quelques</u> amis.** (*He has <u>some [a few]</u> friends.*)

quel The interrogative adjective *quel* is used in subordinate clauses with the subjunctive of the verb *être* (*to be*) introduced by *que* (*qu'*), to mean *whatever*: **<u>Quel que</u> soit votre métier, travaillez bien.** (*<u>Whatever</u> your profession, work well.*) **<u>Quelles que</u> soient ses idées, il est sûr d'avoir tort.** (*<u>Whatever</u> his ideas may be, he is sure to be wrong.*)

tel The adjective *tel(s)*, *telle(s)* (feminine) means *such*; it is often accompanied by the conjunction *que (qu')*, *as*. It is preceded by the indefinite article to mean *such a, such* (plural). In some constructions it is translated as *like, like a*: **Tel est mon avis.** (*Such is my advice.*) **Telles sont ses directives.** (*Such are his instructions.*) **Je n'ai jamais vu un tel film.** (*I never saw such a film.*) **Je ne connais pas de telles personnes.** (*I don't know such people.*) **Une femme telle qu'elle mérite des louanges.** (*A woman like her deserves praise.*)

In noun phrases containing an adjective, *si* or *aussi* is used instead of *tel*: **Avez-vous jamais vu une si belle peinture?** (*Have you ever seen such a beautiful painting?*) **Avez-vous jamais vu d'aussi belles peintures?** (*Have you ever seen such beautiful paintings?*)

tout The adjective *tout* (masculine singular), *tous* (masculine plural), *toute(s)* (feminine) means *each* (indefinite *every*) in the singular, *all* in the plural. Followed by an article or other noun marker, it means *whole* in the singular: **Tout homme a son pays.** (*Every man has his country.*) **Toute femme mérite cela.** (*Every woman deserves that.*) **Tout le pays est fertile.** (*The whole country is fertile.*) **Il a mangé toute une tarte.** (*He ate a whole pie.*) **Presque tous les Français boivent du vin.** (*Nearly all the French drink wine.*)Invariable *tout*, as a pronoun, means *everything*: **Il a tout fait, il a tout vu.** (*He did and he saw everything.*) **Tout est parfait.** *(Everything is perfect.)*

Invariable *tout*, as an adverb, means *entirely* (before a feminine adjective beginning in a consonant or aspirate *h*, the adverb *tout* becomes *toute*): **Nous sommes tout seuls.** (*We're all alone.*) **Elle est tout heureuse.** (*She's completely happy.*) **Elle a été toute surprise et toute honteuse.** (*She was utterly surprised and altogether ashamed.*)

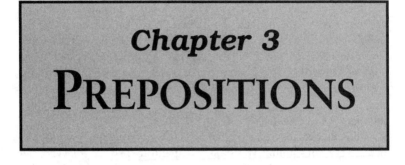

Chapter 3
PREPOSITIONS

In This Chapter:

✔ *General Remarks*
✔ *Indicating Location or Direction*
✔ *With Geographical Names*
✔ *With Modes of Transportation*
✔ *With Expressions of Time*
✔ *Used to Join Two Nouns*
✔ *Introducing the Modifier of an Indefinite Pronoun*
✔ *In Adverb Phrases of Manner*
✔ *Introducing an Infinitive Depending on a Noun or Adjective*

General Remarks

A preposition is an invariable word which introduces an element of a sentence that it unites or subordinates in a certain way to another element of the sentence. Prepositions can establish many kinds of connections or relationships between various parts of a sentence. They can indicate place, time, cause, goal, means, manner, possession, etc.:**Il va <u>à</u> la bibliothèque.** (*He's going <u>to</u> the library.*) **Il habite ici <u>depuis</u> deux ans.** (*He's been living here <u>for</u> two years.*) **Voici le livre <u>de</u> ma mère.** (*Here's my mother<u>'s</u> book.*)

A prepositional locution is a group of words that has the same role as a preposition: **La boutique est <u>en face de</u> l'école.** (*The shop is <u>across from</u> the school.*) **Il travaille <u>afin de</u> vivre.** (*He works <u>in order to</u> live.*)

A difficulty for English speakers is that often a preposition in English has several French counterparts, and the correct translation depends on the meaning in the sentence. For example, the preposition *with* in English can be translated into French in various ways, depending on the context: **Il écrit <u>avec</u> un crayon.** (*He's writing <u>with</u> a pencil.*) **Il écrit <u>de</u> la main gauche.** (*He writes <u>with</u> his left hand.*) **Elle danse <u>de</u> joie.** (*She's dancing <u>with</u> joy.*) **La rue est couverte <u>de</u> feuilles.** (*The street is covered <u>with</u> leaves.*) **Il marche la tête haute.** (*He walks <u>with</u> his head held high.*)

Indicating Location or Direction

à With names of places, *à* can indicate location or direction in, at, or to some place: **Jean est <u>à</u> l'école.** (*Jean is in school.*)**Marie est <u>au</u> bureau.** (*Marie is <u>at</u> the office.*) **Marie va <u>au</u> bureau tous les jours.** (*Marie goes <u>to</u> the office every day.*)

de *De* indicates the place of origin with the verbs *venir, sortir, arriver, s'éloigner, partir,* etc. **Je rentre <u>du</u> bureau.** (*I'm coming home <u>from</u> the office.*) **Ils sortent <u>de</u> la maison.** (*They're going <u>out of</u> the house.*)

dans, en *Dans* (*in, into*) is always used with an article. *En* (*in, into*) is rarely used with an article: **Il entre <u>dans</u> la salle de classe.** (*He's going <u>into</u> the classroom.*)**Il est <u>en</u> classe.** (*He is <u>in</u> class.*)

Dans is used to indicate place more precisely than *à* or *en* and often means the same things as *à l'intérieur de* (*inside*): **Nous allons <u>en</u> ville.** (*We're going <u>into</u> town.*)**Nous allons partout <u>dans</u> la ville.** (*We're going everywhere <u>in</u> the city.*) **Il est**

à la maison? (*Is he at home?*) **Oui, il est dans la cuisine.** (*Yes, he's in the kitchen.*) *Dans* can indicate the place where a thing can be found or where a thing is put: **Il a du chocolat dans la bouche.** (*He has chocolate in his mouth.*) **Il met ses clefs dans sa poche.** (*He puts his keys into his pocket.*) *Dans* is used with the names of streets and avenues, but *sur* is used with the names of boulevards and highways: **Il habite dans l'avenue Foch ou dans la rue de Prony.** (*He lives on avenue Foch or in the rue de Prony.*) **Les enfants ne devraient pas jouer dans la rue.** (*Children should not play in the street.*) **Mon école se trouve sur le boulevard Saint-Michel.** (*My school is on the boulevard Saint-Michel.*)

chez *Chez* (*to, at someone's house, someone's place of business*) is used with a person, a person's name, a pronoun, a person's profession or business, a group, or a society: **Nous allons chez Marie.** (*We're going to Marie's house.*) **Je vais chez le boulanger.** (*I'm going to the baker's.*) **Chez les Américains on est grand.** (*Among Americans people are big.*)

Chez is used with pronouns to mean *at home*: **Faites comme chez vous.** (*Make yourself at home.*)

Chez can also mean *in an author's work*, figuratively speaking: **Chez Molière il y a toutes sortes de monomanes.** (*In Molière's work there are all kinds of monomaniacs.*)

With Geographical Names

à The preposition *à* is used before the names of most cities: **Il va à Paris.** (*He is going to Paris.*) **Il habite à Québec.** (*He lives in Quebec City.*)

The names of a few cities contain a definite article; some are masculine, others are feminine: *à La* is used before feminine names, the contraction *au* before masculine names: **à La Havanne, au Caire** (*in* or *to* Havana, Cairo).

The preposition *à* is also used before the masculine names of many small islands; the article *la* is included before the feminine names of a few small islands. (For exceptions, see *en*): **à Haïti, à la Martinique** (*in* or *to Haiti, Martinique*)

en The preposition *en* is used with feminine names of countries and continents. Almost all names of countries ending in mute *e* are feminine (exception: **le Mexique**): **Je vais en France.** (*I'm going to France.*) **Je**

reste **en** France. (*I'm staying in France.*) **Tu iras en Europe avant d'aller vivre en Afrique.** (*You'll go to Europe before going to live in Africa.*) *En* is used with feminine names of French and Canadian provinces and American states. Almost all French names of provinces and states ending in mute *e* and in *ie* are feminine (but **le Maine**, French province and American state, and **le Nouveau-Mexique**); exception: **à Terre-Neuve** (*in* or *to Newfoundland*): **en Provence, en Californie, en Nouvelle-Ecosse** (*in* or *to Provence, California, Nova Scotia*).

En is also used before the names of some small islands (see also *à*): **en Corse, en Islande** (*in* or *to Corsica, Iceland*).

au(x) The contraction *au* is used with masculine names of countries; more rarely, *aux* is used when the name is plural: **Elle revient aux Etats-Unis.** (*She's coming back to the United States.*) **Philadelphie est aux Etats-Unis.** (*Philadelphia is in the United States.*)

dans When the name of a city or country is accompanied by a modifier, *dans le (la, l', les)* is used instead of *à, en,* or *au(x)*: **J'aimerais vivre dans le Paris des années 20.** (*I would like to live in the Paris of the 20s.*) **Nous allons voyager dans toute la France.** (*We're going to travel in all of France.*)

Dans le (l') is used with masculine names of most French and Canadian provinces and American states; for American states the expression *dans l'état de* is also used. Almost all French names of provinces and states not ending in mute *e* or in *ie* are masculine (but **le Maine, le Nouveau-Mexique**): **dans le Poitou, dans l'Ontario, dans l'état de Kentucky** (*in* or *to Poitou, Ontario, Kentucky*); exceptions: **au Québec** (*in* or *to Quebec*), **au Nouveau-Mexique** (*in* or *to New Mexico*).

de, d' *De* is used to mean *from* before the name of a city and, without a definite article, before the feminine name of a country, province, or state: **Il est de Paris.** (*He is from Paris.*) **Elle revient d'Angleterre.** (*She's coming back from England.*) **Je viens de Caroline du sud.** (*I come from South Carolina.*)

De is used without the definite article to mean *of* before the feminine name of a country, province, or state when it is unmodified: **l'histoire de France, les vins d'Alsace, les ports de l'Espagne médiévale** (*the history of France, the wines of Alsace, the ports of medieval Spain*)

The contraction *des* is used to mean *from* or *of* before plural names of countries: **Il revient des Etats-Unis.** (*He's coming back from the*

United States.) **l'histoire** <u>des</u> **Emirats Arabes Unis** (*the history* <u>*of the*</u> *United Arab Emirates*).

Before the names of cities and islands that contain a definite article, *de La* (feminine) and *du* (masculine) are used to mean *from* or *of*: **de La Mecque, <u>du</u> Puys** (<u>*from*</u> or <u>*of*</u> *Mecca, Le Puys*).

par, pour The prepositions *pour* and *par* are used, with appropriate articles, in certain expressions: **L'avion va <u>partir pour la</u> Martinique.** (*The plane is going <u>to leave for</u> Martinique.*) **<u>En route pour</u> Marseille, elle s'arrête à Lyon.** (<u>*On the way to*</u> *Marseilles, she is stopping at Lyons.*) **Elles veulent <u>passer par</u> Rennes.** (*They want <u>to go by way</u> of Rennes.*)

With Modes of Transportation

à **à bicyclette, <u>à</u> cheval, <u>à</u> motocyclette, <u>à</u> pied, <u>à</u> vélo** (<u>*on a*</u>, <u>*on*</u> or <u>*by*</u> *bicycle, horseback, motorcycle, foot, bike*).

en **<u>en</u> auto, autobus, avion, bateau, métro, taxi, voiture** (<u>*by*</u> *car, bus, plane, boat, subway, taxi, car*).

dans *Dans* is used in expressions for getting into a vehicle or a on ship: **Il monte <u>dans</u> le bus, la voiture, le train.** (*He's getting <u>on</u> the bus, <u>into</u> the car, <u>on</u> the train.*) **Nous embarquons <u>dans</u> le France au Havre.** (*We get <u>on</u> the France at Le Havre.*)

de *De* is used in expressions for getting out of a vehicle or off a ship: **Il descend <u>du</u> bus, <u>de</u> la voiture, <u>du</u> train.** (*He's getting <u>off</u> the bus, <u>out of</u> the car, <u>off</u> the train.*) **Nous débarquons <u>du</u> bateau.** (*We're getting <u>off</u> the boat.*)

With Expressions of Time

à **Il reviendra <u>à</u> cinq heures.** (*He'll return at five o'clock.*)

dans *Dans*, meaning *in*, indicates the time after which a certain thing can be done: **Je le ferai <u>dans</u> une heure.** (*I'll do it <u>in</u> an hour*, that is, after an hour has passed). **L'avion arrive <u>dans</u> dix minutes.** (*The plane arrives <u>in</u> ten minutes.*)

en *En*, meaning *in*, indicates the period during which a certain thing is done: **Je le ferai <u>en</u> une heure.** (*I'll do it <u>in</u> an hour*, that is, it takes me an hour to do it). **Le bateau traverse l'Atlantique <u>en</u> cinq jours.** (*The boat crosses the Atlantic <u>in</u> five days.*)

 avant *Avant* means *before* in reference to time: **Je le ferai <u>avant</u> cinq heures.** (*I'll to it <u>before</u> five o'clock.*) **Elle est arrivée <u>avant</u> Pierre.** (*She arrived <u>before</u> Pierre.*)

 Devant means *before*, *in front of* in reference to space: **Elle était <u>devant</u> Pierre dans la queue.** (*She was <u>before</u> Pierre in the line.*)

 après *Après* means *after* in reference to time: **Je le ferai <u>après</u> cinq heures.** (*I'll do it <u>after</u> five o'clock.*) **Elle est arrivée <u>après</u> Pierre.** (*She arrived <u>after</u> Pierre.*)

 Derrière means *after*, *behind* in reference to space: **Elle était <u>der-</u> <u>rière</u> Pierre dans la queue.** (*She was <u>after</u> Pierre in the line.*)

Used to Join Two Nouns

To indicate function:

à un verre <u>à</u> eau (*a water glass*), **une brosse <u>à</u> dents** (*a toothbrush*).

To join a noun to another noun that modifies it:

de un verre <u>d'</u>eau (*a glass of water*), **mon professeur <u>de</u> maths** (*my math professor*), **une agence <u>de</u> voyage** (*a travel agency*).

To mean *with* when the second noun is considered a distinct part of the first:

à, de une soupe <u>aux</u> pois (*a pea soup*, that is, a soup made with peas), **la glace <u>à</u> la vanille** (*vanilla ice cream*), **du café <u>au</u> lait** (*coffee with milk*). **la fille <u>aux</u> yeux bleus** (*the girl with blue eyes*).

To indicate the material from which a thing is made:

Usage determines whether *de* or *en* is used. Sometimes they are interchangeable: **une robe <u>de</u> soie, <u>en</u> soie** (*a silk dress*), **un sac <u>de</u> cuir, <u>en</u> cuir** (*a leather bag*).

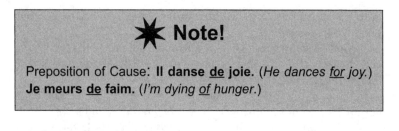

Note!

Preposition of Cause: **Il danse de joie.** (*He dances for joy.*)
Je meurs de faim. (*I'm dying of hunger.*)

Introducing the Modifier of an Indefinite Pronoun

de When *quelque chose* (*something*), *rien* (*nothing*), *quelqu'un* (*someone*) and *personne* (*no one*) are modified by an adjective, the adjective is introduced by *de*; the adjective is always invariable: **Il mange quelque chose de bon.** (*He's eating something good.*) **Personne d'intéressant n'est venu.** (*No one interesting came.*) **Il ne dit rien d'intelligent.** (*He says nothing intelligent.*)

In Adverb Phrases of Manner

à In many adverbial phrases where *in*, *by*, or *on* are used in English, *à* is used in French: **Il parle à voix basse/à haute voix.** (*He speaks in a low voice/out loud.*) **Ce pullover est fait à la main.** (*This sweater is made by hand.*) **Le train arrive à l'heure.** (*The train will arrive on time.*)

de *De* introduces a noun accompanied by the indefinite article: **Il me regarde d'un air furieux.** (*He looks at me with a furious expression.*) **Elle le fait d'une manière adroite.** (*She does it skillfully.*)

avec *Avec* often introduces a noun not accompanied by the indefinite article: **Il parle avec faiblesse.** (*He speaks weakly.*) **Il me regarde avec fureur.** (*He looks at me furiously.*) **Elle le fait avec adresse.** (*She does it skillfully.*)

Introducing an Infinitive Depending on a Noun or Adjective

à

- To indicate the function of a noun or the use to which a thing is destined: **du papier à écrire** (*writing paper*), **une machine à laver** (*a washing machine*), **une chambre à coucher** (*a bedroom*), **de l'eau à boire** (*drinking water*).

- To describe a noun in terms of a possible result: **une tâche à vous rendre fou** (*a job that can drive you crazy*), **un exercice à recopier** (*an exercise to copy over again*).

- To introduce an infinitive that intensifies the meaning of an adjective: **un insecte laid à faire peur** (*an insect ugly enough to scare you*).

- To introduce an infinitive indicating the action to which an adjective applies: **C'est facile à faire.** (*It's easy to do.*) **C'est bon à manger.** (*It's good to eat.*)

- To introduce an infinitive after an expression of duration, length of time, or position of the body: **Il passe son temps à travailler.** (*He spends his time working*) **Elle est debout à travailler.** (*She is working standing up.*) **Il met longtemps à décider.** (*It takes him a long time to decide.*)

de

- To express most other relationships between a noun or an adjective and an infinitive: **Je suis heureux d'être ici.** (*I'm happy to be here.*) **Il avait raison de faire cela.** (*He was right to do that.*) **Il est nécessaire d'étudier.** (*It's necessary to study.*)

Chapter 4
NUMBERS, DATES, TIME

✔ *Numbers*
✔ *Dates*
✔ *Time*

Numbers

Cardinal Numbers

The cardinal numbers in French are:

1-10: un, deux, trois, quatre, cinq, six, sept, huit, neuf, dix

11-19: onze, douze, treize, quatorze, quinze, seize, dix-sept, dix-huit, dix-neuf

20-30: vingt, vingt et un, vingt-deux, vingt-trois, vingt-quatre, vingt-cinq, vingt-six, vingt-sept, vingt-huit, vingt-neuf, trente

40-41, 50-51: quarante, quarante et un; cinquante, cinquante et un

60-61: soixante, soixante et un

70-79: soixante-dix, soixante et onze, soixante-douze, soixante-treize, soixante-quatorze, soixante-quinze, soixante-seize, soixante-dix-sept, soixante-dix-huit, soixante-dix-neuf

80-89: quatre-vingts, quatre-vingt-un, quatre-vingt-deux, quatre-vingt-trois, quatre-vingt-quatre, quatre-vingt-cinq, quatre-vingt-six, quatre-vingt-sept, quatre-vingt-huit, quatre-vingt-neuf

90-99: quatre-vingt-dix, quatre-vingt-onze, quatre-vingt-douze, quatre-vingt-treize, quatre-vingt-quatorze, quatre-vingt-qinze, quatre-vingt-seize, quatre-vingt-dix-sept, quatre-vingt-dix-huit, quatre-vingt-dix-neuf

100-105: cent, cent un, cent deux, cent trois, cent quatre, cent cinq

200-203: deux cents, deux cent un, deux cent deux, deux cent trois

1000-1004: mille, mille un, mille deux, mille trois, mille quatre

1200-1201: mille deux cents, mille deux cent un/douze cents, douze cent un

2000-2002: deux mille, deux mille un, deux mille deux

1948: mille neuf cent quarante-huit/dix-neuf cent quarante-huit

1 000 000, 2 000 000: un million, deux millions

1 000 000 000: un milliard

1 000 000 000 000: un billion

Remember!

In the formation of numbers from 70 through 99, a system based on 20 replaces the one based on 10. In Belgium and Switzerland, but never in the standard language of France, the 10-based system is maintained: 70 **septante**, 71 **septante et un**, 72 **septante-deux**, etc.; 80 **octante** (rarely **huitante**), etc.; 90 **nonante**, etc.

- In the numbers 21, 31, 41, 51, 61, and 71 the conjunction *et* is used and in writing there is no hyphen.
- In 81 and 91 *et* is not used; these numbers are written with hyphens.
- In 101, 1001, etc., neither *et* occurs nor are the numbers written with hyphens.
- When *vingt, cent, million, milliard*, etc., are multiplied and no other number follows them, they become plural: **quatre-vingts, deux cents, deux millions, six milliards, trois billions**.
- When another number follows, the *-s* is not written: **quatre-vingt-trois, deux cent un, deux million trois cent mille**.
- *Mille* is invariable.

- In long numbers, such as dates, *mille* is usually written as *mil*.
- When 1, 21, 31, 41, 51, and 61 are used with a feminine noun, the form **une** is used: **une fille, vingt et une filles, cent une filles**.
- *Million, milliard, billion, trillion*, are treated like expressions of quantity and take the preposition *de* before nouns: **un million d'hommes, un milliard de francs, un trillion de dollars**.
- Contrary to American usage, *un milliard* is a billion, *un billion* a trillion, *un trillion* a quadrillion.
- In France a period or, increasingly in printed texts, a space is used in long numbers where, in the United States, a comma is found: **2.000.000 de francs, 2 000 000 d'habitants**.
- In France a comma is used in fractions where a period is used in the United States and Canada: **3,5 degrés**.

Ordinal Numbers

Ordinal numbers are formed by adding the suffix *-ième* to the cardinal number. If the cardinal number ends in mute *e*, the *e* is dropped: **deuxième, troisième, vingt et unième, quatre-vingt-onzième, deux cent quatrième, millième**.

An adjustment in spelling is required for *cinq*: **cinq > cinquième**.

Three ordinals are irregular: **un, une > premier, première; deux > second, seconde; neuf > neuvième**.

The ordinals *deuxième* and *second* are interchangeable, but *second* is preferred when there are only two of a thing,

A fourth irregular ordinal, *tiers*, feminine *tierce*, is used instead of *troisième* in certain fixed expressions (*tiers* is also used as the fraction): **le tiers état** (*the third estate*), **un tiers/une tierce** (*a third party*).

Collective Numbers

To express an approximate quantity, the suffix *-aine* is added to the cardinal number. One such expression, *une douzaine*, has a quite specific meaning. (Note that in spelling, the final mute *e* is dropped before the suffix and *x* is changed to *z* in *dizaine*.) Collective numbers function like expressions of quantity: **Je voudrais une dizaine de pêches.** (*I'd like ten or so peaches.*) **Prends une douzaine d'œufs.** (*Take a dozen eggs.*) **Il a acheté cinq douzaines d'œufs.** (*He bought five dozen eggs.*) **Il a lu neuf centaines de livres.** (*He has read about 900 books.*)

You Need to Know ✔

The Use of Ordinals with Cardinals

In the titles of rulers, the ordinal *Premier, Première* is used for the first in succession, and the cardinal in all other cases: **Napoléon I**ᵉʳ (= **Napoléon Premier**) (*Napoleon I*), **Elisabeth I**ʳᵉ (= **Elisabeth Première**) (*Elizabeth I*), **Elisabeth II** (= **Elisabeth Deux**) (*Elizabeth II*) **Jean XXIII** (= **Jean Vingt-Trois**) (*John XXIII*). When a cardinal and an ordinal are used together, the cardinal comes first, contrary to English usage: **les deux premières semaines de mars** (*the first two weeks of March*), **les trois derniers jours des vacances** (*the last three days of vacation*).

The irregular form *un millier* ("about a thousand") may be pluralized like *douzaine* and *centaine*: **J'ai cinq milliers de dollars.** (*I have around $5,000.*) **Cela coûte des milliers de francs.** (*That costs thousands of francs.*)

Other expressions, such as *à peu près* (*nearly*), *environ* (*about*), and *dans les* (in speaking of money or age) may be used instead of collective numbers: **Il y a une trentaine d'élèves dans sa classe/Il y a à peu près trente élèves dans sa classe/Il y a environ trente élèves dans sa classe.** (*There are about thirty pupils in his class.*)

A collective number with the definite article implies a person's age: **Il a passé la cinquantaine.** (*He is past his fiftieth birthday.*) **Ils ont célébré sa soixantaine.** (*They celebrated her sixtieth birthday.*)

Fractions

Normally, the cardinal number and the ordinal number are used together to form fractions (note the plurals): 1/5 (**un cinquième**), 3/5 (**trois cinquièmes**), 5/8: (**cinq huitièmes.**)

Three fractions are irregular (note that *quart* has a plural form): 1/2 (**un demi**), 1/3 (**un tiers**), 1/4 (**un quart**), 6 1/2 (**six et demi**), 7 2/3 (**sept et deux tiers**), 9 3/4 (**neuf et trois quarts**).

The expression *et demi* follows the noun; *demi* functions as an adjective, so it is *demie* in the feminine: **L'enfant a un an et demi.** (*The child is one and a half years old.*) **Jean a vingt ans et demi.** (*Jean is twenty and a half.*) **J'ai bu une bouteille et demie de vin.** (*I drank a bottle and a half of wine.*)

The expression *la moitié de* is also used for *half of* a specific thing: **J'ai bu la moitié d'une bouteille.** (*I drank half a bottle.*) **Il dort la moitié du temps.** (*He sleeps half the time.*) **Il a mangé la moitié de la dinde.** (*He ate half of the turkey.*)

Invariable *demi-* may precede the noun as a prefix to indicate a specific quantity: **Je voudrais une demi-douzaine de pommes.** (*I'd like a half-dozen apples.*) **Je reviens dans une demi-heure.** (*I'll be back in a half hour.*)

Calculations

The verb *faire* (*to do, to make*) is used in arithmetic operations. Notice that the plural *font* is used for addition, subtraction, and multiplication, while the singular *fait* is used for division: **Addition: 3 et 3 font 6** (*three and/plus three are six.*) **Subtraction: 5 moins 1 font 4** (*five minus one makes four.*) **Multiplication: 5 fois 10 font 50** (*five times 10 are 50.*) **Division: 10 divisé par 2 fait 5** (*ten divided by 2 makes 5.*)

Dimensions

Length, width, height, and depth are expressed in the following ways: **Ce mur est long de cinq mètres (5 m)/Ce mur a cinq mètres (5 m) de long/Ce mur a cinq mètres (5 m) de longueur.** (*This wall is five meters long.*) **Ce mur est haut de 5 m./Ce mur a 5 m de haut /Ce mur a 5 m de hauteur.** (*This wall is five meters high.*) **Cette table est large d'un mètre et demi (1 m 50)/Cette table a 1 m 50 de large (de largeur).** (*This table is one and a half meters wide.*) **La piscine est profonde de 3 m./La piscine a 3 m de profondeur.** (*The pool is three meters deep.*)

Dates

Days of the Week and Months of the Year

Note that the days of the week and months of the year are not capitalized in French:

Days of the week: **lundi** (*Monday*), **mardi** (*Tuesday*), **mercredi** (*Wednesday*), **jeudi** (*Thursday*), **vendredi** (*Friday*), **samedi** (*Saturday*), **dimanche** (*Sunday*)

Months of the year: **janvier** (*January*), **février** (*February*), **mars** (*March*), **avril** (*April*), **mai** (*May*), **juin** (*June*), **juillet** (*July*), **août** (*August*), **septembre** (*September*), **octobre** (*October*), **novembre** (*November*), **décembre** (*December*)

How to Ask What the Date Is

Quel jour est-ce aujourd'hui?/Quel jour sommes-nous aujourd'hui? (*What day is it today?*) **Quelle est la date aujourd'hui?** (*What is the date today?*)

How to Give the Date

Dates are given with the definite article *le* followed by the cardinal number, except for the first of the month when the ordinal *premier* is used (note the two styles for giving the year): **C'est aujourd'hui lundi /Nous sommes aujourd'hui lundi.** (*Today is Monday.*) **C'est aujourd'hui le cinq mai.** (*Today is May 5.*) **C'est aujourd'hui le lundi cinq mai.** (*Today is Monday, May 5.*) **On célèbre la Fête du travail le premier mai.** (*Labor Day is celebrated May 1.*) **C'est aujourd'hui le samedi vingt et un août mil neuf cent quatre-vingt-dix-neuf.** [formal style]/**C'est aujourd'hui le samedi vingt et un août dix-neuf cent quatre-vingt-dix-neuf.** [informal style] (*Today is Saturday, August 21, 1999.*)

Other Useful Expressions

L'hiver commence en décembre. (*Winter begins in December.*) **Je suis né au mois d'avril.** (*I was born in (the month of) April.*)

Time

In France clock time is expressed in both a familiar and an official style.

Familiar Conversational Style

In everyday conversation, the 24-hour day is divided into two 12-hour segments. Minutes from 1 to 14 and 16 to 29 are expressed in cardinal numbers that follow the expression for the hour; minutes from 31 to 44 and 46 to 59 are subtracted from the following hour. Quarter after the hour is expressed as *et quart*; quarter to an hour is expressed as *moins le quart* or *moins un quart*. The half-hour is expressed as *et demie*. As the words for hour (*heure*) and minute (*minute*) are feminine, the numerals for "one" and "twenty-one" are *une* and *vingt et une*. In this style, *midi* is used for 12:00 noon and *minuit* for 12:00 midnight; as these expressions are masculine, the masculine form *demi* is used: **Il est une heure.** (*It is one o'clock.*) **Il est deux heures et quart.** (*It is two fifteen.*) **Il est six heures vingt et une.** (*It is six twenty-one.*) **Il est neuf heures et demie.** (*It is nine thirty.*) **Il est dix heures moins vingt.** (*It is nine forty/twenty to ten.*) **Il est midi moins dix.** (*It is ten to twelve noon.*) **Il est minuit une.** (*It is one past midnight.*) **Il est minuit et demi.** (*It is twelve thirty a.m.*)

To specify periods of the day, adverbial phrases are used with expressions using *heure(s)*: **Je suis invité pour trois heures de l'après-midi.** (*I'm invited for three o'clock in the afternoon/at three p.m.*) **Nous partons à huit heures moins le quart du soir.** (*We leave at seven forty-five in the evening/at 7:45 p.m.*) **Je me suis enfin endormi à deux heures du matin.** (*I finally got to sleep at two in the morning/at two a.m.*)

Official Style

Official time in France is based on the 24-hour system like military time. It is used in formal announcements and in schedules and time tables. Numbers are used for all hours and all parts of the hour. Adverbial phrases clarifying the period of the day would be redundant: **Le train arrive à 0 h (à zéro heure).** (*The train arrives at midnight.*) **L'avion décolle à 12 h 35 (à douze heures trente-cinq).** (*The plane takes off at 12:35 p.m.*) **Le film commence à 21 h 45 (à vingt et une heures quarante-cinq).** (*The movie starts at 7:45 p.m.*) **On l'a arrêté à 23 h 15 (à vingt-trois heures quinze).** (*He was arrested at 11:15 p.m.*)

Chapter 5
VERBS

IN THIS CHAPTER:

✔ *Persons of the Verb and Personal Pronouns*
✔ *The Verb System*
✔ *Simple Tenses*
✔ *Compound Tenses*
✔ *Uses of the Infinitive*
✔ *The Passive Voice*

French verbs at first appear to be difficult to the native English speaker, but they are really not so difficult as they appear. Each verb is not unique; many verbs that are formed in the same way can be grouped together in classes or conjugations. This fact greatly facilitates learning verb forms. As you will observe in subsequent parts of this chapter, even many so-called irregular verbs have characteristics in common and thus can be grouped together.

Persons of the Verb and Personal Pronouns

In French, unlike other Romance languages, personal pronouns must be used as the subject of a verb unless a noun or another pronoun takes its place.

There are four ways to express *you*. To address a friend, a young child, a relative or close associate, the "familiar" pronoun *tu* (the 2nd singular form) is used. To address anyone else, the "formal" pronoun *vous* (the 2nd plural form) is used as a singular. To address two or more people, whether familiarly or formally, *vous* is used as a plural form.

The 3rd singular pronoun *on* is an impersonal pronoun meaning *one, people (in general)*, and *we, you,* or *they* in general, not specific senses.

The subject personal pronouns are:

	singular	plural
1st person	**je** (**j'** before a vowel or mute *h*)	**nous**
2nd person	**tu**	**vous**
3rd person	**il** (masculine)	**ils**
	elle (feminine)	**elles**
	on (impersonal)	

The Verb System

Verb tenses in French occur in simple and in compound forms. To form simple tenses, personal endings are added to verb stems; to form compound tenses, an auxiliary verb—either *avoir* (*to have*) or *être* (*to be*)— is combined with a past participle.

Simple Tenses: present indicative, present subjunctive, past subjunctive, imperfect, imperfect subjunctive, future, present conditional, *passé simple*

Compound Tenses: passé composé, plus-que-parfait, passé antérieur, pluperfect subjunctive, future perfect, conditional perfect (or past conditional)

You Need to Know ✔

The *passé simple* (simple past), the *passé antérieur* (a past perfect), the imperfect subjunctive, and the *passé antérieur* subjunctive are "literary" tenses that are found only in formal writing. They are no longer used in the spoken language, in informal writing such as personal letters, or in literary writing that imitates informal usage.

The *passé composé* (compound past) is a present perfect; however, in the spoken language and in informal writing, it is also—and primarily—used to replace the *passé simple* as a past indefinite (which expresses a single action in the past without implying duration or repetition).

The *plus-que-parfait* is a past perfect used both in informal and in formal speaking and writing.

The imperative (used to give commands), the infinitive, and the present and past participles are simple forms; the past infinitive is a compound form.

The infinitive is the form of a verb you will find in a dictionary.

Simple Tenses

The Present Tense

With the exception of four or five highly irregular verbs, all French verbs use one of the following sets of personal endings in the present indicative (note that the plural endings are alike in both sets):

	Set 1		Set 2	
	singular	plural	singular	plural
1st	**-e**	**-ons**	**-s**	**-ons**
2nd	**-es**	**-ez**	**-s**	**-ez**
3rd	**-e**	**-ent**	**-t**	**-ent**

Verbs that use Set 1 do so without variation. Some variations occur in verbs that use Set 2.

In speech, the endings of the singular forms and the 3rd plural forms of both are not pronounced (the 3rd plural and the singular endings in Set 1 are like mute -*e*'s); in all of these forms, a stress accent falls on the verb stem. In the 1st and 2nd plural of both sets the spoken stress falls on the ending and not on the stem. Historically, vowels in French change in different ways depending upon whether they are stressed or unstressed; sometimes the quality of a vowel affects as well the consonant preceding it. This explains why many verbs have different vowels and sometimes different consonants in their stems, and it explains why, in those irregular verbs, the stems for the 1st and 2nd plural are identical and why the stems for the singular forms and the 3rd plural also tend to be alike.

One form of the present tense in French translates into English both as "he does something" and "he is doing something," as well as, in the interrogative, "is he doing something?" and "does he do something?"

Regular Verbs: The First Conjugation

With one exception (the irregular verb *aller*, "to go"), all verbs with infinitives ending in -*er* belong to the First Conjugation. The stem of First Conjugation verbs is found by dropping the -*er* ending. The present indicative is formed by adding Set 1 endings to the stem: **parler** (*to speak*): **je parle**; **tu parles**; **il, elle, on parle**; **nous parlons**; **vous parlez**; **ils, elles parlent**.

habiter (*to live in*): **j'habite**; **tu habites**; **il, elle, on habite**; **nous habitons**; **vous habitez**; **ils, elles habitent**.

First Conjugation Verbs with Spelling Changes

Verbs with Infinitives Ending in -*cer* and -*ger*

The present stems of these verbs end in "soft *c*" (pronounced like *s*) and "soft *g*" (pronounced like *g* in *mirage*). In French spelling, *c* and *g* followed by *a*, *o*, or *u* are "hard"—"hard *c*" is pronounced like *k*, "hard *g*" is pronounced like *g* in English *girl*. When verb endings beginning in *a* or *o* are added to stems ending in "soft *c*" or "soft *g*," spelling changes are introduced to show that the consonants are "soft"; *c* becomes *ç* ("*c* cedilla"), *g* becomes *ge*: **avancer** (*to advance*): **nous avançons, nager** (*to swim*): **nous nageons.**

Verbs with -*é*- as the Last Vowel in the Stem

In conjugating verbs with –*é*- as last vowel in the stem, the vowel changes to –*è*- in those forms where it is stressed (1st, 2nd, 3rd singular, 3rd plural); *é* remains when the endings are stressed (1st and 2nd plural): **compléter** (*to complete*): **je complète; tu complètes; il, elle, on complète; nous complétons; vous complétez; ils, elles complètent.**

Verbs with "Mute *e*" as the Last Vowel in the Stem

In conjugating verbs with "mute *e*" as the last vowel in the stem—that is, an -*e*- without an accent mark—, spelling changes are introduced in forms where it is stressed to indicate a change in pronunciation from "mute *e*," a neutral vowel that is often not pronounced at all, to an open *e* (similar to the *e* in English *best*).

The most common way to show the open vowel is to change "mute *e*" to *è*: **lever** (*to raise*): **je lève; tu lèves; il, elle, on lève; nous levons; vous levez; ils, elles lèvent.**

Other such verbs are: **acheter** (*to buy*), **geler** (*to freeze*), **amener** (*to bring, lead in*), **mener** (*to lead*), **élever** (*to raise*), **peser** (*to weigh*), **emmener** (*to take, lead away*), **promener** (*to walk, to take for a walk*), **enlever** (*to take away*).

In a few verbs, the consonant following "mute *e*" is doubled: **jeter** (*to throw*): **je jette; tu jettes; il, elle, on jette; nous jetons; vous jetez; ils, elles jettent.**

Other such verbs are **appeler** (*to call*), **rappeler** (*to call back, to remind*), and derivatives of *jeter* like **projeter** (*to project*) and **rejeter** (*to reject*).

Verbs with –*y*- as the Last Letter in the Stem

Verbs with infinitives ending in -*yer* have a semi-consonant (similar to *y* in English *yes*) before accented endings (1st and 2nd plural), but in standard French the semi-consonant does not occur before endings that are not stressed. In the 1st, 2nd, 3rd singular and 3rd plural, -*y*- changes to *-i-*: **payer** (*to pay, pay for*): **je paie; tu paies; il, elle, on paie; nous payons; vous payez; ils, elles paient.**

Regular Verbs: The Second Conjugation

Many verbs with infinitives ending in *-ir* are in the Second Conjugation. The present stem is found by dropping the *-ir*. The present tense is formed by adding Set 2 endings with the infixes *-i-* in the singular and *–iss-* in the plural: **finir** (*to finish*): **je finis; tu finis; il, elle, on finit; nous finissons; vous finissez; ils, elles finissent.**
Many Second Conjugation verbs are built upon adjectives: cf. *jaunir* (*to become yellow*) from *jaune*; *verdir* (*to become green*) from *vert*.

Haïr (*to hate*) is like a Second Conjugation verb except for the singular forms in the present indicative, where the vowel sound is *ai* (pronounced as one syllable) rather than *aï*, spelled with a dieresis (¨) (pronounced as two syllables). Note that *haïr* begins with "aspirate *h*": **je hais; tu hais; il, elle, on hait; nous haïssons; vous haïssez; ils, elles haïssent.**

Dormir (*to sleep*), *sentir* (*to feel, to smell*), etc. constintute a group of verbs are related to the Second Conjugation, but they differ in two respects: (1) they are conjugated with Set 2 endings, but do not take the *–i-*, *-iss-* infixes; (2) the last consonant in the stem disappears in the singular: **dormir** (*to sleep*): **je dors; tu dors; il, elle, on dort; nous dormons; vous dormez; ils, elles dorment.**

sentir (*to feel, to smell*): **je sens; tu sens; il, elle, on sent; nous sentons; vous sentez; ils, elles sentent.**

servir (*to serve*): **je sers; tu sers; il, elle, on sert; nous servons; vous servez; ils, elles servent.**

Other verbs in this group include: **endormir** (*to put to sleep*), **repartir** (*to leave again*), **mentir** (*to tell a lie*), **se repentir** (*to repent*), **partir** (*to leave, to depart*), **sortir** (*to go out*).

Regular Verbs: The Third Conjugation

Many verbs with infinitives ending in *-re*, and most ending in *-dre*, are in the Third Conjugation. The present stem is found by dropping *-re*.

The present tense is formed by adding Set 2 endings to the stem. If the stem ends in *d*, as is the case with most verbs in the Third Conjugation, the *t* is not added in the 3rd singular; however, in all cases when the *d* is pronounced it is sounded as a *t*: **répondre** (*to answer*): **je répond̲s̲**; **tu répond̲s̲**; **il, elle, on répond**; **nous répond̲o̲n̲s̲**; **vous répond̲e̲z̲**; **ils, elles répond̲e̲n̲t̲**.

Rompre and its derivatives are regular Third Conjugation verbs: **rompre** (*to break*): **je romp̲s̲**; **tu romp̲s̲**; **il, elle, on romp̲t̲**; **nous romp̲o̲n̲s̲**; **vous romp̲e̲z̲**; **ils, elles romp̲e̲n̲t̲**.

Derivatives of *rompre* include **corrompre** (*to corrupt*), **interrompre** (*to interrupt*).

Conclure is like a Third Conjugation except in the *passé simple*:
conclure (*to conclude*): **je conclu̲s̲**; **tu conclu̲s̲**; **il, elle, on conclu̲t̲**; **nous conclu̲o̲n̲s̲**; **vous conclu̲e̲z̲**; **ils, elles conclu̲e̲n̲t̲**.

The following verbs are conjugated like *conclure*: **exclure** (*to exclude*), **inclure** (*to include*)

Battre is a Third Conjugation verb; however, in the singular and 3rd plural the double *t* in the stem reduces to a one *t* in the singular and the ending *t* is not added in the 3rd singular: **battre** (*to beat*): **je ba̲t̲s̲**; **tu ba̲t̲s̲**; **il, elle, on ba̲t̲**; **nous batt̲o̲n̲s̲**; **vous batt̲e̲z̲**; **ils, elles batt̲e̲n̲t̲**.

Derivatives of *battre* include **abattre** (*to slaughter*), **combattre** (*to combat*), **débattre** (*to debate*).

Mettre is also a Third Conjugation verb like *battre*: **mettre** (*to put*): **je me̲t̲s̲**; **tu me̲t̲s̲**; **il, elle, on met**; **nous mett̲o̲n̲s̲**; **vous mett̲e̲z̲**; **ils, elles mett̲e̲n̲t̲**.

Derivatives of *mettre* include **admettre** (*to admit*), **promettre** (*to promise*), **omettre** (*to omit*), **remettre** (*to put back, to remit*), **permettre** (*to permit*), **soumettre** (*to submit*).

Rire (*to laugh*) and its derivative **sourire** (*to smile*) resemble Third Conjugation Verbs in the simple tenses: **rire** (*to laugh*): **je ri̲s̲**; **tu ri̲s̲**; **il, elle, on ri̲t̲**; **nous ri̲o̲n̲s̲**; **vous ri̲e̲z̲**; **ils, elles ri̲e̲n̲t̲**.

Vaincre (*to conquer*) and its derivative **convaincre** (to convince) have two irregularities: (1) the *-t* is not added in the 3rd singular and (2) in spelling *-c-* changes to *-qu-* (also pronounced like *k*) in the plural: **je vaincs; tu vaincs; il, elle, on vainc; nous vainquons; vous vainquez; ils, elles vainquent.**

Irregular Verbs

Cueillir, Ouvrir, etc.

A few common verbs with infinitives ending in *-ir* are conjugated by adding Set 1 endings to the stem: **ouvrir** (*to open*): **j'ouvre; tu ouvres; il, elle, on ouvre; nous ouvrons; vous ouvrez; ils, elles ouvrent.**

Verbs conjugated like *ouvrir* include: **accueillir** (*to welcome*), **cueillir** (*to pick, to gather*), **recueillir** (*to collect*), **offrir** (*to offer*), **couvrir** (*to cover*), **recouvrir** (*to cover again*), **découvrir** (*to discover*), **souffrir** (*to suffer*).

Courir and its derivatives
Although the infinitive of *courir* ends in *-ir*, it is otherwise like a Third Conjugation Verb: **courir** (*to run*): **je cours; tu cours; il, elle, on court; nous courons; vous courez; ils, elles courent.**

Derivatives of *courir* include: **parcourir** (*to pass over, through*), **recourir** (*to rerun, to have recourse*), **secourir** (*to come to the aid of*).

Connaître (*to know someone*), *paraître* (*to seem, to appear*), *naître* (*to be born*), etc.
These verbs and their derivatives have certain similarities with *haïr* (see above). The stem is found by dropping *-tre* and removing the circumflex accent: **connaître** (*to know someone*): **je connais; tu connais; il, elle, on connaît; nous connaissons; vous connaissez; ils, elles connaissent.**

Common derivatives of these verbs include **apparaître** (*to appear*), **disparaître** (*to disappear*), **reconnaître** (*to recognize*), **renaître** (*to be reborn*).

Plaire (*to be pleasing*), *déplaire* (*to displease*), and *se taire* (*to keep quiet*)

These verbs are similar to *connaître*, except that single *s* (pronounced like *z*) rather than double *s* (pronounced like *s*) occurs in the plural. Note that the circumflex accent is not used in the infinitives or in the 3rd singular of *se taire*: **plaire** (*to be pleasing*): **je plais; tu plais; il, elle, on plaît; nous plaisons; vous plaisez; ils, elles plaisent.**

Lire (*to read*), *dire* (*to say*), **conduire** (*to drive, to conduct*) and other verbs with infinitives ending in *-ire*

Unlike *rire*, which is like a Third Conjugation verb throughout the present (see above), these verbs resemble Third Conjugation verbs in the singular, but in the plural a single *s* (pronounced like *z*) is added before the endings. Note that *dire* has an irregular form in the 2nd plural (*vous dites*); however, in the derivatives of *dire* the 2nd plural form is like that of the other verbs (e.g., *vous médisez, vous interdisez*). The stem is found by removing the *-re* in the infinitive: **lire** (*to read*): **je lis; tu lis; il, elle, on lit; nous lisons; vous lisez; ils, elles lisent; dire** (*to say*): **je dis; tu dis; il, elle, on dit; nous disons; vous dites; ils, elles disent.**

Common verbs in this class include **conduire** (*to drive, to conduct*), **construire** (*to construct*), **cuire** (*to cook*), **détruire** (*to destroy*), **élire** (*to elect*), **interdire** (*to forbid*), **médire** (*to slander*), **maudire** (*to curse*), **nuire** (*to do harm*), **produire** (*to produce*), **réduire** (*to reduce*), **suffire** (*to suffice*), **traduire** (*to translate*).

Ecrire (*to write*), *vivre* (*to live*), *suivre* (*to follow*) and their derivatives

These verbs take Set 2 endings, but *v* is inserted in the plural. The stem is found by removing *-(v)re* from the infinitive: **écrire** (*to write*): **j'écris; tu écris; il, elle, on écrit; nous écrivons; vous écrivez; ils, elles écrivent.**

Common derivatives of these verbs include **décrire** (*to describe*), **inscrire** (*to inscribe, to enroll*), **poursuivre** (*to pursue*), **récrir** (*to rewrite*), **survivre** (*to survive*).

Prendre (*to take*) and its derivatives

These verbs resemble verbs of the Third Conjugation; however, the *d* of the stem disappears in the plural. Note the double *n* in the 3rd plural, a sign that the vowel (corresponding to the mute *e* of the 1st and 2nd plural) is stressed in this form: **je prends; tu prends; il, elle, on prend; nous prenons; vous prenez; ils, elles prennent.**

Common derivatives of *prendre* include **apprendre** (*to learn, to teach*), **comprendre** (*to understand*), **surprendre** (*to surprise*), **méprendre** (*to misunderstand*), **reprendre** (*to take back*).

Croire (*to believe*), *fuir* (*to flee*), *voir* (*to see*) and their derivatives
These verbs are not unlike First Conjugation verbs with infinitives ending in *–yer* in that the *i* of the stem changes to *y* in the 1st and 2nd plural; however, the endings are Set 2. The stem is found by removing *-r(e)* from the infinitive: **croire** (*to believe*): **je crois; tu crois; il, elle, on croit; nous croyons; vous croyez; ils, elles croient.**
Common derivatives of these verbs include **prévoir** (*to foresee*), **revoir** (*to see again*), **s'enfuir** (*to run away*).

Craindre (*to fear*), *joindre* (*to join*), *peindre* (*to paint*), and similar verbs
These verbs have stems that end in *n*, which is not pronounced following the nasal vowel in the singular. The plural stem contains palatal *n* (similar to *ny* in English *canyon*), which is spelled *gn*; in pronunciation the vowel is denasalized in the plural. To form the present, Set 2 endings are added to the stem, which is found by removing *-dre* from the infinitive: **craindre** (*to fear*): **je crains; tu crains; il, elle, on craint; nous craignons; vous craignez; ils, elles craignent.**
joindre (*to join*): **je joins; tu joins; il, elle, on joint; nous joignons; vous joignez; ils, elles joignent.**
Other verbs in this group include **atteindre** (*to reach, to attain*), **dépeindre** (*to depict*), **éteindre** (*to extinguish*), **plaindre** (*to pity*), **rejoindre** (*to join, to rejoin*), **repeindre** (*to repaint*).

Venir (*to come*), *tenir* (*to hold*), and their derivatives
These verbs have a vowel change from *e* in the forms where the ending is stressed to *ie* in the forms where the stem is stressed. Like the vowels in verbs like *craindre* and *prendre* (above), *ie* is nasal in the singular forms. Note the double *n* in the 3rd plural, a sign that the vowel, like the vowel in *prendre*, is open and stressed: **venir** (*to come*): **je viens; tu viens; il, elle, on vient; nous venons; vous venez; ils, elles viennent.**
These verbs' many derivatives include **appartenir** (*to belong*), **contenir** (*to contain*), **convenir** (*to be convenient, to befitting*), **devenir** (*to become*), **maintenir** (*to maintain*), **obtenir** (*to obtain*), **parvenir** (*to reach, to attain*), **redevenir** (*to become again*), **retenir** (*to retain*), **revenir** (*to come back*), **soutenir** (*to uphold*), **se souvenir** (*to remember*).

Acquérir (*to acquire*) and **conquérir** (*to conquer, to win*)
In spelling these verbs have a vowel change similar to that of *venir, tenir*, etc. However, the last vowel in the stem when the ending is stressed is *é*, not mute *e*. Note that the stressed vowel is spelled *è* in the 3rd plural: **j'acquiers; tu acquiers; il, elle, on acquiert; nous acquérons; vous acquérez; ils, elles acquièrent**.

Pouvoir (*to be able to, can, may*) and *vouloir* (*to want, to wish*)
Like some of the verbs above with nasal and denasalized vowels, these verbs actually have three stems: one for the singular, one for the 1st and 2nd plural, and one for the 3rd plural; the 3rd plural has the vowel of the singular forms plus the consonant introduced in the 1st and 2nd plural. The stem that is obtained when -*oir* is removed from the infinitive is the stem characteristic of the 1st and 2nd plural. Note that in these verbs, *x* replaces the *s* of the 1st and 2nd singular endings: **pouvoir** (*to be able to*): **je peux; tu peux; il, elle, on peut; nous pouvons; vous pouvez; ils, elles peuvent**.
vouloir (*to want*): **je veux; tu veux; il, elle, on veut; nous voulons; vous voulez; ils, elles veulent**.

Pleuvoir (*to rain*) is conjugated like *pouvoir*, but is used only in the 3rd singular: **il pleut** (*it is raining*)

Mourir (*to die*) has a similar vowel change: **je meurs; tu meurs; il, elle, on meurt; nous mourons; vous mourez; ils, elles meurent**.

Devoir (*to owe, to have to, must*), **recevoir** (*to receive*), and similar verbs
These verbs have three stems in a pattern similar to *pouvoir* and *vouloir*, except that the vowel changes from mute *e* to *oi*. Notice that in verbs in -*cevoir* the cedilla is used before *o*; just like *c* before *e*, *ç* is pronounced like *s*: **devoir** (*to owe*): **je dois; tu dois; il, elle, on doit; nous devons; vous devez; ils, elles doivent**.
recevoir (*to receive*): **je reçois; tu reçois; il, elle, on reçoit; nous recevons; vous recevez; ils, elles reçoivent**.
Verbs conjugated like *recevoir* include **apercevoir** (*to perceive, to catch sight of*), **concevoir** (*to conceive*), **décevoir** (*to disappoint*).

Boire (*to drink*) also has three stems; the vowel change is from *u* to *oi*: **je bois**; **tu bois**; **il, elle, on boit**; **nous buvons**; **vous buvez**; **ils, elles boivent**.

Valoir (*to be worth*) has two stems. Note the use of *x* rather than *s* in the 1st and 2nd singular: **je vaux**; **tu vaux**; **il, elle, on vaut**; **nous valons**; **vous valez**; **ils, elles valent**.

Falloir (*to be necessary*) is conjugated like *valoir*, but is used only in the 3rd singular: **il faut**.

Avoir (*to have*), *être* (*to be*), *aller* (*to go*), *faire* (*to make, to do*), and *savoir* (*to know a fact, to know how to*) are highly irregular: **avoir** (*to have*): **j'ai**; **tu as**; **il, elle, on a**; **nous avons**; **vous avez**; **ils, elles ont**; **être** (*to be*): **je suis**; **tu es**; **il, elle, on est**; **nous sommes**; **vous êtes**; **ils, elles sont**.

faire (*to make, to do*): **je fais**; **tu fais**; **il, elle, on fait**; **nous faisons**; **vous faites**; **ils, elles font**.

aller (*to go*): **je vais**; **tu vas**; **il, elle, on va**; **nous allons**; **vous allez**; **ils, elles vont**.

savoir (*to know*): **je sais**; **tu sais**; **il, elle, on sait**; **nous savons**; **vous savez**; **ils, elles savent**.

Special Uses of the Present Indicative

The present tense in French is used the same as in English to express an action that is going on in the present. As in English, the present tense is also used to express habitual actions taking place in the present or a permanent situation. In French only the form of the simple present is used; forms of a present tense with special helping verbs such as *to be* or *to do* are unknown in French: **Elle dort maintenant.** (*She is sleeping now.*) **Tous les matins ils vont à l'école.** (*Every morning they go to school.*) **La neige est froide.** (*Snow is cold.*)

To insist on the duration of an action in the present, use *être en train de* followed by an infinitive: **Il est en train de s'habiller.** (*He's getting dressed.*) **Je suis en train d'étudier maintenant.** (*I'm studying right now.*)

The present tense can be used to express the immediate future: **Il arrive dans cinq minutes.** (*He arrives/will arrive in five minutes.*)

A special use of the time expressions *depuis, il y a . . . que*, and *voilà . . . que* expresses an action that began in the past and continues into the present. In English the present perfect is used, in French it is the present: **Depuis quand attend-il?** *(How long has he been waiting?)* **Il attend depuis une semaine/ Voilà une semaine qu'il attend/Il y a une semaine qu'il attend**. *(He has been waiting for a week.)*

Depuis can also mean *for* (a period of time) or *since* (a date or time): **Depuis quand vient-il ici?** *(How long has be been coming here?)* **Il vient depuis novembre.** *(He's been coming since November.)***Depuis combien de temps vient-il ici?** *(For how long has he been coming here?)* **Il vient depuis trois ans.** *(He's been coming for three years.)*

Remember!

Clock time can sometimes be ambiguous: *deux heures* can mean two hours or two o'clock. To be precise, use *depuis* for clock time and *il y a . . . que* or *voilà . . . que* for a number of hours: **J'attends depuis une heure.** *(I've been waiting since one o'clock.)* **Voilà une heure que j'atttends.** *(I've been waiting for an hour.)*

The idiom *venir de* used in the present tense and followed by an infinitive means *to have just done something*: **Nous venons de dîner.** *(We have just had dinner.)*

Reflexive or Pronominal Verbs

The action of a reflexive (or a pronominal) verb is both executed and received by the subject. Since the subject receives the action, a pronoun complement called the reflexive pronoun is used. In English reflexive pronouns are *myself, yourself, himself, herself, itself, ourselves*, etc.: **Je me regarde dans le miroir.** *(I look at myself in the mirror.)*

Pronominal verbs sometimes indicate reciprocal action: **Nous nous aimons.** (*We love each other/one another*) **Ils se marient.** (*They are getting married.*)

Many, perhaps most, reflexive verbs in French are not translated as reflexives in English.

Note that mute *e* in reflexive pronouns elides with a vowel or mute *h*: **se réveiller** (*to wake up*): **je me réveille; tu te réveilles; il, elle, on se réveille; nous nous réveillons; vous vous réveillez; ils, elles se réveillent.**

s'habiller (*to get dressed*): **je m'habille;tu t'habilles; il, elle, on s'habille; nous nous habillons; vous vous habillez; ils, elles s'habillent.**

Many actions can be done to oneself or to someone else: **Je me réveille à six heures.** (*I wake up at six o'clock.*) **Je réveille les enfants à six heures.** (*I wake the children up at six.*)

S'asseoir (*to sit down*) is an irregular reflexive verb; it refers to the action of sitting down, not to the state of being seated: **je m'assieds; tu t'assieds; il, elle, on s'assied; nous nous asseyons; vous vous asseyez; ils, elles s'asseyent.**

Reflexive Verbs with Parts of the Body

Consistent with the rule that possessive adjectives are not used with parts of the body when the meaning is clear (Chap. 3), the definite article is used when parts of the body are used with reflexive verbs: **Je me lave la figure.** (*I am washing my face.*)

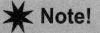

✳ Note!

Reflexive Verbs in the Infinitive

The reflexive pronoun always precedes the infinitive. Note that the pronoun agrees with the subject of the clause: **Je vais me promener.** (*I'm going to take a walk.*) **Ils veulent se coucher.** (*They want to go to bed.*) **Vous pouvez vous asseoir.** (*You may sit down.*)

Imperative

The imperative mood is used to give commands. In French there are three forms of the imperative: 2nd singular (familiar), 1st plural, and 2nd plural (familiar plural, formal singular and plural). In most verbs, the imperative form is like the indicative form. Notice, however, that in all -*er* verbs, including *aller*, the -*s* is dropped from the 2nd singular: **parler** (*to speak*): **parle** (*speak*), **parlons** (*let us speak*), **parlez** (*speak*); **finir** (*to finish*): **finis** (*finish*), **finissons** (*let us finish*), **attendre** (*to wait*): **attends** (*wait*), **attendons** (*let us wait*), **attendez** (*wait*). **aller** (*to go*): **va** (*go*), **allons** (*let us go*), **allez** (*go*). **Parle français, s'il te plaît.** (*Speak French, please.*) **Finissons notre travail.** (*Let's finish our work.*) **Vendez votre automobile.** (*Sell your car.*) **Ecrivez à votre grand-mère.** (*Write your grandmother.*)

In -*er* verbs, when the 2nd singular form is followed by the pronouns *en* or *y*, which are joined to the imperative by a hyphen, -*s* is restored: **Vas-y!** (*Go there!*) **Achètes-en une douzaine.** (*Buy a dozen of them.*)

The imperative of four verbs is irregular (these forms are related to the subjunctive): **avoir** (*to have*): **aie** (*have*), **ayons** (*let us have*), **ayez** (*have*); **être** (*to be*): **sois** (*be*), **soyons** (*let us be*), **soyez** (*be*); **savoir** (*to know*): **sache** (*know*), **sachons** (*let us know*), **sachez** (*know*); **vouloir** (*to wish, to want*): **veuille** (*please*), **veuillez** (*please*) (the 1st plural is lacking) (This imperative of *vouloir* is used in very formal circumstances only.) **Aie pitié des pauvres.** (*Take pity on the poor.*)**Soyons raisonnables!** (*Let's be reasonable!*)**Sachez que je vous aime.** (*Know that I love you.*) **Veuillez ne pas fumer.** (*Please do not smoke.*)

The Affirmative Imperative of Reflexive Verbs

In the affirmative imperative, the reflexive pronoun follows the verb and is joined to it by a hyphen. Note that *te* is replaced by *toi* except before the pronouns *en* and *y*, when *te* becomes *t'*: **se lever** (*to get up*): **lève-toi** (*get up*), **levons-nous** (*let us get up*), **levez-vous** (*get up*). **Amuse-toi bien.** (*Have a really good time.*) **Achète-t'en deux.** (*Buy two of them for yourself.*) **Dépêchez-vous!** (*Hurry up!*)

The Negative Imperative

The imperative is made negative by placing the negative particle *ne* before the verb—*n'* before a vowel or mute *h*—and *pas* following the verb: **Travaille.** >**Ne travaille pas.** **Ecoutons.** > **N'écoutons pas.**

The Negative Imperative of Reflexive Verbs

In the negative imperative of reflexive verbs, the reflexive pronoun precedes the verb. Note that the 2nd singular form is *te* (*t'*): **Habille-toi.** > **Ne t'habille pas.** **Lève-toi.** > **Ne te lève pas.** **Dépêchons-nous.** > **Ne nous dépêchons pas.**

The Present Participle

Formation

In nearly all verbs the present participle is formed by dropping the ending *-ons* from the 1st plural form of the present indicative and adding the ending *–ant*: **nous parlons** > **parlant, nous avançons** > **avançant, nous mangeons** > **mangeant, nous finissons** > **finissant, nous répondons** > **répondant, nous dormons** > **dormant, nous craignons** > **craignant**

Only *avoir*, *être*, and *savoir* have irregular stems (except for *être*, these forms are related to the subjunctive and the imperative forms). **nous avons** > **ayant, nous sommes** > **étant, nous savons** > **sachant**

Use of the Present Participle

When the present participle is used as an adjective, it agrees in number and gender with the noun it modifies: **La fille souriante est très jolie.** (*The smiling girl is very pretty.*) **Il parle d'une voix menaçante.** (*He speaks with a menacing voice.*)

The present participle is invariable when it is used to express an action that takes place at the same time as the action of the principle verb: **J'ai trouvé mes freres faisant la cuisine.** (*I found my brothers cooking.*) **Finissant son travail, il ferme son livre.** (*Finishing his work, he closes his book.*)

A participle phrase may be used to express cause: **Etant profes-seur, il veut enseigner.** (*Since he is a professor, he wants to teach.*) **Sachant la vérité, elle peut maintenant se reposer.** (*Knowing the truth, she can rest now.*)

The present participle is frequently used after the preposition *en* to mean *while, upon* or *by* doing something; reinforced by the adverb *tout*, *en* may mean *although*: **On apprend en étudiant.** (*People learn by studying.*) **En me promenant, j'ai aperçu Jean.** (*While walking, I caught sight of Jean.*) **En arrivant, j'ai vu Marie.** (*Upon arriving I saw Marie.*) **Tout en vous aimant, je reconnais vos défauts.** (*Although I love you, I recognize your faults.*)

After any preposition other than *en*, the infinitive is used in French instead of the present participle: **Elle a commencé par faire l'appel.** (*She began by calling the roll.*) **Il part sans dire au revoir.** (*He leaves without saying goodbye.*) **Brosse-toi les dents avant de te coucher.** (*Brush your teeth before going to bed.*)

The Imperfect Tense

Formation

The imperfect tense is formed using the same stem as the present participle—that is, dropping the *-ons* ending from the 1st plural form of the present indicative—and adding the following endings:

	singular	plural
1st person	**-ais**	**-ions**
2nd person	**-ais**	**-iez**
3rd person	**-ait**	**-aient**

Notice the similarities with Set 2 endings. Despite spelling differences, the singular endings and the 3rd plural are pronounced alike: **parler** (*to speak*), present participle: **parlant**: **je parlais; tu parlais; il, elle, on parlait; nous parlions; vous parliez; ils, elles parlaient.**

finir (*to finish*), present participle: **finissant**: **je finissais; tu finissais; il, elle, on finissait; nous finissions; vous finissiez; ils, elles finissaient.**

recevoir (*to receive*), present participle: **recev~~ant~~**: je recev<u>ais</u>; tu recev<u>ais</u>; il, elle, on recev<u>ait</u>; nous recev<u>ions</u>; vous recev<u>iez</u>; ils, elles recev<u>aient</u>.

être (*to be*), present participle: **ét~~ant~~**: j'ét<u>ais</u>; tu ét<u>ais</u>; il, elle, on ét<u>ait</u>; nous ét<u>ions</u>; vous ét<u>iez</u>; ils, elles ét<u>aient</u>.

> *Avoir* and *savoir* have imperfect stems formed not from the present participle, which is irregular, but from the 1st plural: **avoir** (*to have*), 1st plural: **nous av~~ons~~**: j'av<u>ais</u>; tu av<u>ais</u>; il, elle, on av<u>ait</u>; nous av<u>ions</u>; vous av<u>iez</u>; ils, elles av<u>aient</u>;
> **savoir** (*to know*), 1st plural: **nous sav~~ons~~**: je sav<u>ais</u>; tu sav<u>ais</u>; il, elle, on sav<u>ait</u>; nous sav<u>ions</u>; vous sav<u>iez</u>; ils, elles sav<u>aient</u>.

Avancer, **manger**, and other First Conjugation verbs with spelling changes before *-ons* and *-ant* keep *ç* and *ge* before the endings beginning in *a*, but drop the changes before endings beginning in *i*.

avancer (*to advance*), present participle: **avan<u>çant</u>**: j'avan<u>ç</u>ais; tu avan<u>ç</u>ais . . . ; nous avan<u>c</u>ions; vous avan<u>c</u>iez . . . .

manger (*to eat*), present participle: **mang<u>eant</u>**: je mang<u>e</u>ais; tu mang<u>e</u>ais . . . ; nous mang<u>ions</u>; vous mang<u>iez</u> . . . .

Uses of the Imperfect Tense

Continuing Action

The imperfect tense describes activities in the past. It indicates actions begun in the past but not necessarily completed at a given point in time. It expresses past actions that are habitual or customary. Some common adverbs and adverbial expressions that indicate continuance and frequency are: **toujours** (*always*), **souvent** (*often*), **fréquemment** (*frequently*), **parfois** (*sometimes*), **d'habitude** (*usually*), **quelquefois** (*sometimes*), **bien des fois** (*often, many times*), **de temps en temps** (*from time to time*), **en ce temps-là** (*at that time, during that time*), **tous les jours** (*everyday*), **tous les lundis**, etc. (*every Monday*, etc.), **le lundi**, etc. (*on Mondays*, etc.), **chaque jour, mois, année** (*every day, month, year*).

There are many ways to translate the imperfect into English:
Elles mangeaient toujours dans ce restaurant. (*They always used to eat in this restaurant.*) **Il venait me voir fréquemment.** (*He came to see me frequently.*) **Je jouais souvent au football.**(*I would play football often.*)

The imperfect is used to describe what people were doing rather than report what people did: **Ils bavardaient pendant que les filles chantaient.** (*They were talking while the girls were singing.*)

The imperfect is used to describe what was going on when something happened: **J'étudiais quand le téléphone a sonné.** (*I was studying when the phone rang.*)

Description

The imperfect is used to describe conditions or circumstances that were in existence when specific actions occurred. It is also used to designate conditions in the past that no longer exist: **Il faisait beau.** (*The weather was nice.*) **Il pleuvait.** (*It was raining.*) **Elle portait une blouse bleue.** (*She was wearing a blue blouse.*) **Vous aviez de la chance.** (*You were lucky.*) **Le Louvre était le palais des rois de France.** (*The Louvre was the palace of the kings of France.*)

Mental Activity, Emotional States, etc.

Since most mental processes involve duration or continuance, verbs denoting mental activities and conditions are frequently used in the imperfect in reference to the past: **Je ne voulais pas partir.** (*I didn't want to leave.*) **Nous pouvions venir le samedi.** (*We could come on Saturdays.*) **Il ne savait pas les réponses.** (*He did not know the answers.*) **Elle croyait que j'avais raison.** (*She thought that I was right.*) **A quoi pensaient-ils?** (*What were they thinking about?*)

Si and the Imperfect

Si (*if, if only, what if,* etc.) is used with the imperfect, often as a question, to express a wish or, especially with *on* and *nous*, to form a kind of imperative: **Si on jouait au tennis?** (*How about playing tennis?*) **Si nous allions au cinéma?** (*Suppose we went to the movies?*) **Ah, si j'étais riche!** (*If only I were rich!*)

Depuis, il y a ... que, **and** *voilà ... que*

A special use of the time expressions *depuis, il y a
... que,* and *voilà ... que* expresses an action that
began at some time in the past and continued until
another event in the past. In English the past perfect
is used, in French it is the imperfect. Compare this
usage with the use of the present indicative with
depuis, il y a, etc. (above): **Depuis quand**

attendait-il? (*How long had he been waiting?*)**Il attendait depuis une
semaine/Voilà une semaine qu'il attendait/Il y a une semaine qu'il
attendait.** (*He had been waiting for a week.*)

    Depuis can also mean *for* (a period of time) or *since* (a date or
time): **Depuis quand venait-il ici?** (*How long had be been coming
here?*) **Il venait depuis novembre.** (*He had been coming since
November.*) **Depuis combien de temps venait-il ici?** (*For how long had
he been coming here?*) **Il venait depuis trois ans.** (*He had been coming for three years.*)

    Clock time can sometimes be ambiguous: *deux heures* can mean
two hours or two o'clock. To be precise, use *depuis* for clock time and
il y a ... que or *voilà ... que* for a number of hours: **J'attendais depuis une heure.** (*I'd been waiting since one o'clock.*) **Voilà une heure
que j'atttendais.** (*I had been waiting for an hour.*)

Venir de with the Imperfect

The idiom *venir de* used in the imperfect tense and followed by an
infinitive means *to have just done something* before another event in the
past. Compare with the use of the present with *venir de* (above).
Nous venions de dîner. (*We had just had dinner.*)

The Future

Immediate Future with *aller*

The immediate future can be expressed by using the verb *aller* followed
by an infinitive. This is the equivalent of English "going to do." **Je vais
travailler ici.** (*I'm going to work here.*) **Nous allons dîner à huit
heures.** (*We are going to have dinner at 8:00.*)

The Future Tense: Formation

Regular Stems

The future tense of most verbs is formed by adding the following endings to the infinitive. These endings resemble the present indicative of *avoir*. Notice in Third Conjugation verbs and other verbs with infinitives ending in -*re*, the final *e* is dropped before the future endings.

	singular	*plural*
1st person	-ai	-ons
2nd person	-as	-ez
3rd person	-a	-ont

parler (*to speak*): je parler**ai**; tu parler**as**; il, elle, on parler**a**; nous parler**ons**; vous parler**ez**; ils, elles parler**ont**.

finir (*to finish*): je finir**ai**; tu finir**as**; il, elle, on finir**a**; nous finir**ons**; vous finir**ez**; ils, elles finir**ont**.

attendre (*to wait*): j'attendr**ai**; tu attendr**as**; il, elle, on attendr**a**; nous attendr**ons**; vous attendr**ez**; ils, elles attendr**ont**.

The future tense of most irregular verbs has the same formation: **rire, sourire**> je rir**ai**, etc.; **suivre, poursuivre** > je suivr**ai**, etc.; **mettre, permettre**, etc. > je mettr**ai**, etc.; **prendre**, etc. > je prendr**ai**, etc.; **dire, médire**, etc. > je dir**ai**, etc.; **écrire, décrire**, etc. > j'écrir**ai**, etc.; **conduire, traduire**, etc. > je conduir**ai**, etc.; **connaître, paraître**, etc. > je connaîtr**ai**, etc.; **boire, croire** > je boir**ai**, etc.; **lire, élire**, etc. > je lir**ai**, etc.; **vivre, survivre, revivre** > je vivr**ai**, etc.; **ouvrir, couvrir**, etc. > j'ouvrir**ai**, etc.; **craindre, plaindre** > je craindr**ai**, etc.

With one exception, all classes of First Conjugation verbs with changes in the present stem incorporate into the infinitive the stem common to the singular and 3rd plural forms before adding the future endings. This is because in pronunciation a secondary accent falls on the stem.

lever: je lèverai, tu lèveras, il lèvera, nous lèverons, vous lèverez, ils lèveront;

jeter: je jetterai, tu jetteras, il jettera, nous jetterons, etc.

payer: je paierai, tu paieras, il paiera, etc., nous paierons, etc.

(*Envoyer* [*to send*] and its derivatives have an irregular future stem: envoyer: **j'enverrai, tu enverras, il enverra,** etc.)

The exceptional class includes all verbs with *é* as the last vowel in the present stem. The *é* is maintained in spelling, although the vowel change is observed in pronunciation: **céder: je céderai, tu céderas, il cédera, nous céderons, vous céderez, ils céderont.**

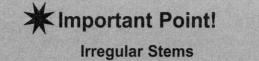

✴ Important Point!

Irregular Stems

Some verbs have irregular future stems that, in many cases, are recognizable as deformations of the basic infinitive.
cueillir: je cueillerai, etc.; **s'asseoir: je m'assiérai,** etc.; **faire: je ferai,** etc.; **avoir: j'aurai,** etc.; **savoir: je saurai,** etc.; **falloir: il faudra; valoir: je vaudrai,** etc.; **vouloir: je voudrai,** etc.; **recevoir: je recevrai,** etc.; **devoir: je devrai,** etc.; **pleuvoir: il pleuvra; courir: je courrai,** etc.; **mourir: je mourrai,** etc.; **pouvoir: je pourrai,** etc.; **voir: je verrai,** etc.; **tenir: je tiendrai,** etc.; **venir: je viendrai,** etc.; **être: je serai,** etc.; **aller: j'irai,** etc.

The Future Tenses: Uses

The future tense is used primarily to discuss events lying in the future and to speculate about those events: **Pourront-ils finir à l'heure?** (*Will they be able to finish on time?*) **Vous ferez le voyage en avion.** (*You'll make the trip by plane.*) **Ils sauront la vérité.** (*They'll find out the truth.*) **Il ne pleuvra pas demain.** (*It won't rain tomorrow.*)

Contrary to English usage, the future tense is used after certain subordinating conjunctions when the verb in the main clause is in the future; futurity is implicit in the dependent clause. The following conjunctions are typical: **quand, lorsque, au moment où** (*when*); **dès que, aussitôt que** (*as soon as*); **pendant que, tandis que** (*while*). **Je le verrai quand il arrivera.** (*I'll see him when he arrives.*) **Je vous appellerai au moment où il arrivera.** (*I will call you the moment he arrives.*) **Nous dînerons aussitôt que la viande sera cuite.** (*We'll have* *dinner as soon as the meat is cooked.*) **Pendant que le garçon jouera de la guitare les filles chanteront.** (*While the boy plays the guitar the girls will sing.*) Often the imperative also implies futurity: **Dites-moi quand il arrivera.** (*Tell me when he arrives.*) **Parlons à Jean dès qu'il arrivera.** (*Let's talk to Jean as soon as he arrives.*)

The Present Conditional

Formation

Without exception the conditional is formed by adding the endings for the imperfect to the stem used for the future.

parler (*to speak*): **je parlerais; tu parlerais; il, elle, on parlerait; nous parlerions; vous parleriez; ils, elles parleraient.**

finir (*to finish*): **je finirais; tu finirais; il, elle, on finirait; nous finirions; vous finiriez; ils, elles finiraient.**

attendre (*to wait*): **j'attendrais; tu attendrais; il, elle, on attendrait; nous attendrions; vous attendriez; ils, elles attendraient.**

lever: je lèverais, etc.; **jeter: je jetterais,** etc.; **payer: je paierais,** etc.; **céder: je céderais,** etc.; **cueillir: je cueillerais,** etc.; **avoir: j'aurais,** etc.; **recevoir: je recevrais,** etc.; **courir: je courrais,** etc.; **envoyer: j'enverrais,** etc.; **tenir: je tiendrais,** etc.; **être: je serais,** etc.

Uses of the Conditional

Conditions Contrary to Fact and Similar Constructions
See *Si* **Clauses** (below).

Courteous Requests

In polite usage, the conditional is used to soften a request, a command, or an expression of the speaker's desire. Very often the verbs used are *pouvoir* (*can, may*) and *vouloir* (*to wish, to want*): **Pourriez-vous m'aider?** (*Could you help me?*) **Auriez-vous la gentillesse de me dire où se trouve la gare?** (*Would you have the kindness to tell me where the station is?*) **Je voudrais vous en parler.** (*I'd like to speak to you about it.*)

After Certain Conjunctions

Parallel to usage in the future, the conditional is used after *quand, lorsque, dès que, aussitôt que* and *tant que* when the main verb is in the conditional: **Il mangerait quand il arriverait.** (*He would eat when he arrives.*) **Il ferait le travail dès qu'il reviendrait.** (*He would do the work as soon as he came back.*)

Indirect Discourse

The conditional is used to express a future action in indirect discourse when the main verb is in a past tense: **Il m'a dit qu'il viendrait.** (*He told me that he would come.*) **Je me demandais s'il voyagerait en France.** (*I wondered whether he would travel to France.*) **Nous croyions qu'elle voudrait nous rendre visite.** (*We thought that she would want to visit us.*)

To Express Possibility or Uncertainty

This usage is related to indirect discourse as it implies a speech act; the construction is typical of journalistic style: **Il serait à Montréal aujourd'hui.** (*He is rumored to be in Montreal today.*) **Il aurait une peinture de Braque.** (*He allegedly has a Braque painting.*)

The Verb *devoir*

Devoir is often used to express necessity. In the present conditional, it expresses moral obligation: **Il doit travailler** (*He must work*). **Je devrais étudier ce soir.** (*I ought to study this evening.*) **On devrait aider les pauvres.** (*People should help the poor.*)

The Past Participle

Formation: Regular Verbs

The past participle is formed by adding endings to the same stem as used for the present indicative (the infinitive minus *-er, -ir, -re*):
First Conjugation: **parler > parlé;**

Second Conjugation and related verbs: **finir** > **fini**, **haïr** > **haï**, **dormir** > **dormi**;

Third Conjugation and related verbs: **attendre** > **attendu**, **conclure** > **conclu**, **battre** > **battu**, **vaincre** > **vaincu**.

Formation: Irregular Verbs

- Past participles ending in **-i**: **rire**, **sourire** > **ri**, **souri**; **fuire**, **enfuire** >**fui**, **enfui**; **suffire** > **suffi**; **nuire** > **nui**; **suivre**, **poursuivre** > **suivi**, **poursuivi**.
- Past participles ending in **-is**: **mettre**, **permettre**, etc. > **mis**, **permis**, etc.; **prendre**, **comprendre**, etc. > **pris**, **compris**, etc.; **acquérir**, **conquérir** > **acquis**, **conquis**; (**s'**)**asseoir** > **assis**.
- Past participles ending in **-it**: **dire**, **médire**, **maudire**, etc. > **dit**, **médit**, **maudit**, etc.; **écrire**, **décrire**, etc. > **écrit**, **décrit**, etc.
- Past participles ending in **-uit**: **cuire** > **cuit**; **conduire**, **introduire**, etc. > **conduit**, **introduit**, etc.; **construire**, **détruire**, etc. > **construit**, **détruit**, etc.
- Past participles ending in **-u**: **connaître**, **paraître**, etc. > **connu**, **paru**, etc.; **venir**, **tenir**, etc. > **venu**, **tenu**, etc.; **courir**, **secourir**, etc. > **couru**, **secouru**, etc.; **plaire**, **taire**, etc. > **plu**, **tu**, etc.; **décevoir**, **recevoir**, etc. > **déçu**, **reçu**, etc.; **devoir** > **dû** (note the circumflex accent); **boire**, **croire** > **bu**, **cru**; **savoir**, **falloir**, **valoir**, **voir** > **su**, **fallu**, **valu**, **vu**; **vouloir** > **voulu**; **lire**, **élire**, **relire** > **lu**, **élu**, **relu**; **vivre**, **survivre**, **revivre** > **vécu**, **survécu**, **revécu**.
- Past participles ending in **-ert**: **ouvrir**, **couvrir**, etc. > **ouvert**, **couvert**, etc.; **offrir**, **souffrir** > **offert**, **souffert**;
- Past participles of verbs with infinitives ending in *-indre*: **craindre**, **plaindre** > **craint**, **plaint**; **atteindre**, **éteindre**, **peindre** > **atteint**, **éteint**, **peint**; **joindre**, **rejoindre**, etc. > **joint**, **rejoint**.
- Other irregular past participles: **avoir** > **eu**; **être** > **été**; **faire**, **défaire**, **refaire**, etc. > **fait**, **défait**, **refait**, etc.; **mourir** > **mort**; **naître** > **né**.

The *Passé Simple* or Literary Past Tense

Formation: Regular Verbs

The *passé simple* has a basic set of endings, but *-er* verbs (First Conjugation and *aller*) have a special variation. Notice the circumflex

You Need to Know ✔

Uses of the Past Participle

The past participle can be used as an adjective. In this case it agrees in number and gender with the noun it modifies: **C'est une robe faite à la main.** (*It is a hand-made dress.*) **Ce sont des femmes bien aimées.** (*They are well-beloved women.*) **Les fenêtres sont ouvertes.** (*The windows are open.*) The past participle is also used to form compound tenses (below).

accent in the 1st and 2nd plural; it is added to the "theme vowel" that immediately precedes the ending. The "theme vowel" in -*er* verbs is *a*.

	Basic		-*er* Verbs Only	
	singular	plural	singular	plural
1st	-s	^-mes	-ai	-âmes
2nd	-s	^-tes	-<u>as</u>	-âtes
3rd	-t	-rent	-a	-<u>èrent</u>

The stem of the *passé simple* is derived from the past participle. In regular verbs, this stem is found by removing the final vowel from the past participle.

First Conjugation and aller: **parler** (*to speak*), past participle: **parlé**: **je parlai; tu parlas; il, elle, on parla; nous parlâmes; vous parlâtes; ils, elles parlèrent.**

  aller (*to go*), past participle: **allé: j'allai; tu allas; il, elle, on alla; nous allâmes; vous allâtes; ils, elles allèrent.**

  In the Second and Third Conjugation and most related verbs, the "theme vowel" *i* is added to the stem before the basic endings:

Second Conjugation and related verbs: **finir** (*to finish*), past participle:

fini: **je fin**i**s**; **tu fin**i**s**; **il, elle, on fin**i**t**; **nous finîmes**; **vous fin**î**tes**; **ils, elles fin**i**rent**.

haïr (*to hate*), past participle: **haï** (note spelling of 1st and 2nd plural): **je haïs**; **tu haïs**; **il, elle, on haït**; **nous haïmes**; **vous haïtes**; etc.

dormir (*to sleep*), past marticiple: **dormi**: **je dorm**i**s**, **tu dorm**i**s**, etc.

Third Conjugation and related verbs: **attendre** (*to wait for*), past participle: **attendu**: **j'attend**i**s**; **tu attend**i**s**; **il, elle, on attend**i**t**; **nous attend**î**mes**; **vous attend**î**tes**; **ils, elles attend**i**rent**.

battre (*to beat*), past participle: **battu**: **je batt**i**s**; etc.

vaincre (*to conquer*), past participle: **vaincu** (note the spelling change: the final consonant in the stem is pronounced *k* rather than *s*): **je vainqu**i**s**; **tu vainqu**i**s**; **il, elle, on vanqu**i**t**; **nous vainqu**î**mes**; etc.

conclure (*to conclude*), past participle: **conclu** (note that *conclure* and *inclure* have *u* as the theme vowel): **je concl**u**s**, etc.

Formation: Irregular Verbs

In most irregular verbs, the basic endings are added to the past participle ending in *i* or *u*. In these verbs the formation of the *passé simple* may be considered to be regular.

- Past participles ending in -**i**: **rire**, past participle: **ri** > **je r**i**s**, **tu r**i**s**, **il r**i**t**, **nous r**î**mes**, **vous r**î**tes**, **ils r**i**rent**; **fuire**, etc., past participle: **fui** > **je fu**i**s**, etc.; **suffire**, past participle: **suffi** > **je suff**i**s**, etc.; **suivre**, past participle: **suivi**, etc. > **je suiv**i**s**, etc.

- Past participles ending in -**u**: **connaître**, past participle: **connu** > **je conn**u**s**, **tu conn**u**s**, **il conn**u**t**, **nous conn**û**mes**, **vous conn**û**tes**, **ils conn**u**rent**; **paraître**, past participle: **paru** > **je par**u**s**, etc.; **courir**, past participle: **cour**u > **je cour**u**s**, etc.; **plaire**, past participle: **plu** > **je pl**u**s**, etc.; **se taire**, past participle: **tu** > **je me t**u**s**, etc.; **décevoir**, past partivciple: **déçu** > **je déç**u**s**, etc.; **recevoir**, past participle: **reçu** > **je reç**u**s**, etc.; **devoir**, past participle: **dû** > **je d**u**s**, **tu d**u**s**, **il d**u**t**, **nous d**û**mes**, **vous d**û**tes**, **ils d**u**rent**; **boire**, past participle: **bu** > **je b**u**s**, etc.

  croire, past participle: **cru** > **je cr**u**s**, etc.; **savoir**, past participle: **su** > **je s**u**s**, etc.; **falloir**, past participle: **fallu** > **il fall**u**t**; **valoir**, past participle: **valu** > **je val**u**s**, etc.; **vouloir**, past participle: **voulu** > **je**

voulus, etc.; **lire**, past participle: **lu** > **je lus**, etc.; **vivre**, past participle: **vécu** > **je vécus**, etc.; **avoir**, past participle: **eu** > **j'eus**, etc.

In many verbs with past participles ending in **-is** and **-it**, the *passé simple* stem is formed by removing the final consonant and adding the basic endings. This formation is regular.

• Past participles ending in **-is**: **mettre**, past participle: **mis** >**je mis, tu mis, il mit, nous mîmes, vous mîtes, il mirent**; **prendre**, past participle: **pris**, etc. > **je pris, tu pris, il prit**, etc.; **acquérir**, past participle: **acquis** >**j'acquis, tu acquis, il acquit**, etc.; **conquérir**, past participle: **conquis** > **je conquis, tu conquis, il conquit**, etc.; **s'asseoir**, past participle: **assis** > **je m'assis, tu t'assis, il s'assit**, etc.

• Past participles ending in **-it**: **dire**, past participle: **dit** > **je dis, tu dis, il dit, nous dîmes, vous dîtes, ils dirent**.

Other verbs have irregular *passé simple* stems; a few can be classified.

• Past participles ending in **-uit**: the *passé simple* stem with "theme vowel" ends in **-uisi-**: **cuire**, past participle: **cuit** > **je cuisis, tu cuisis, il cuisit, nous cuisîmes, vous cuisîtes, ils cuisirent**; **conduire**, past participle: **conduit** > **je conduisis**, etc.; **introduire**, past participle: **introduit** > **j'introduisis**, etc.; **construire**, etc., past participle: **construit** > **je construisis**, etc.

• Past participles ending in **–int**: the *passé simple* stem with "theme vowel" ends in **-igni-**: **craindre**, past participle: **craint** > **je craignis, tu craignis, il craignit, nous craignîmes, vous craignîtes, ils craignirent**; **plaindre**, past participle: **plaint** > **je plaignis**, etc.; **atteindre**, past participle: **atteint** > **j'atteignis**, etc.; **peindre**, past participle: **peint** > **je peignis**, etc.; **joindre**, past participle: **joint** > **je joignis**, etc.

• Past participles ending in **-ert**: in these verbs the *passé simple* stem resembles the infinitive; the stem with "theme vowel" ends in **-ri-**: **ouvrir**, past participle: **ouvert** > **j'ouvris, tu ouvris, il ouvrit, nous ouvrîmes, vous ouvrîtes, ils ouvrirent**; **couvrir**, past participle: **couvert** > **je couvris**, etc.; **offrir**, past participle: **offert** > **j'offris**, etc.; **souffrir**, past participle: **souffert** > **je souffris**, etc.

Other irregular verbs have *passé simple* stems that are not always recognizable as related to the past participle. But, in forming the *passé*

simple, the basic endings are added to the stem in the regular way:
écrire, stem: écrivi- > j'évrivi<u>s</u>, tu écrivi<u>s</u>, il écrivi<u>t</u>, nous écri-
vî<u>mes</u>, vous écrivî<u>tes</u>, ils écrivi<u>rent</u>; voir, stem: vi- > je vis, etc.
être, stem: fu- > je fu<u>s</u>, etc.; faire, etc., stem: fi- > je fi<u>s</u>, etc.;
mourir, stem: mouru- > je mouru<u>s</u>, etc.; naître, etc., stem: naqui-
> je naqui<u>s</u>, etc.; venir, stem: vin-: je vin<u>s</u>, tu vin<u>s</u>, il vin<u>t</u>, nous vîn-
<u>mes</u>, vous vîn<u>tes</u>, ils vin<u>rent</u>; tenir, stem: tin- > je tin<u>s</u>, etc.

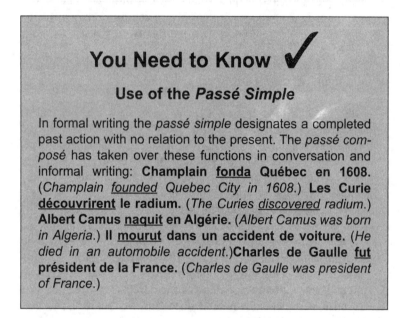

You Need to Know ✔

Use of the *Passé Simple*

In formal writing the *passé simple* designates a completed past action with no relation to the present. The *passé composé* has taken over these functions in conversation and informal writing: **Champlain <u>fonda</u> Québec en 1608.** (*Champlain <u>founded</u> Quebec City in 1608.*) **Les Curie <u>découvrirent</u> le radium.** (*The Curies <u>discovered</u> radium.*) **Albert Camus <u>naquit</u> en Algérie.** (*Albert Camus was born in Algeria.*) **Il <u>mourut</u> dans un accident de voiture.** (*He died in an automobile accident.*)**Charles de Gaulle <u>fut</u> président de la France.** (*Charles de Gaulle was president of France.*)

Compound Tenses

Compound tenses are formed with a conjugated auxiliary verb, either *avoir* or *être* and a past participle. Every simple tense has a corresponding compound tense.

The *Passé Composé*

Formation of the *Passé Composé* with *avoir*

This tense is formed with the present of the auxiliary verb and the past participle. Most verbs have *avoir* as the auxiliary: **parler** (*to speak*): **j'ai parlé**; **tu as parlé**; **il, elle, on a parlé**; **nous avons parlé**; **vous avez parlé**; **ils, elles ont parlé**.

Formation of the *Passé Composé* with *être*

Some verbs have *être* as the auxiliary. Many of these verbs, but not all, are intransitive verbs of motion—that is, in French they do not take direct objects. It is helpful to think of these verbs in pairs of opposites: **aller** (*to go*)—**venir** (*to come*), **entrer** (*to enter*)—**sortir** (*to go out*), **arriver** (*to arrive*)—**partir** (*to leave*), **monter** (*to go up*)—**descendre** (*to go down*), **naître** (*to be born*)—**mourir** (*to die*).

Other verbs in this group include: **rester** (*to stay, to remain*), **tomber** (*to fall*), **retourner** (*to go back*).

Derivatives of these verbs include: **devenir** (*to become*), **ressortir** (*to go back out*), **remonter** (*to go back up*), **retomber** (*to fall back down*), **renaître** (*to be reborn*), **revenir** (*to come back*), **rentrer** (*to return [home]*), **survenir** (*to appear, to happen suddenly*), **repartir** (*to leave again*).

In the *Passé Composé*, as in all compound tenses, the past participle of these verbs conjugated with *être* agrees in number and gender with the subject: **aller** (*to go*): **je suis allé** (male), **je suis allée** (female); **tu es allé** (male), **tu es allée** (female); **il est allé**; **elle est allée**; **nous sommes allés** (male or inclusive group), **nous sommes allées** (female group); **vous êtes allé** (single male, formal), **vous êtes allée** (single female, formal), **vous êtes allés** (male or inclusive group), **vous êtes allées** (female group); **ils sont allés** (male or inclusive group), **elles sont allées** (female group).

mourir (*to die*): **je suis mort, je suis morte; tu es mort, tu es morte; il est mort, elle est morte; nous sommes morts, nous sommes mortes; vous êtes mort, vous êtes morte, vous êtes morts, vous êtes mortes; ils sont morts, elles sont mortes.**

Impersonal *on* can be collective, in which case the past participle does not show agreement, or masculine or feminine plural (in the sense of "we").

Three verbs—*descendre, monter,* and *sortir*—and their derivatives may take either *être* or *avoir* as the auxiliary because they can be used transitively as well as intransitively: **Elle est montée.** (*She went up.*) **Elle a monté l'escalier.** (*She went up the stairs.*) **Elle est descendue.** *She went down.*) **Elle a descendu l'escalier.** (*She went down the stairs.*) **Elle a descendu les valises.** (*She brought the suitcases down.*) **Elle est sortie.** (*She went out.*) **Elle a sorti de l'argent.** (*She got some money out.*)

Agreement of the Past Participle: Verbs Conjugated with *avoir*

The past participle of verbs using *avoir* as the auxiliary agree in number and gender with a preceding direct object: **J'ai écrit une lettre.** (*I wrote a letter.* [no agreement])

In the following examples, the past participle agrees with the relative pronoun *que* which in turn takes its number and gender from its antecedent. No ending is added for masculine singular (note that the relative can be omitted in English, but not in French): **C'est l'homme qu'il a vu.** (*That's the man he saw.*) **Voilà la lettre que j'ai écrite.** (*There's the letter that I wrote.*) **J'adore les photos que tu a prises.** (*I love the photos that you took.*) **les hommes que j'ai craints** (*the men whom I feared*)**la femme qu'il a aimée** (*the woman he loved*)

In the masculine plural, no ending is added when the past participle ends in *–s*: **Les livres qu'il a pris sont ici.** (*The books he took are here.*)

Agreement is shown when the interrogative adjective is used: **Quelles photos as-tu prises?** (*Which photos did you take?*) **Quels hommes a-t-il craints?** (*What men did he fear?*)

Finally, agreement is shown with personal pronoun direct objects (*See* Chap. 8).

Pronominal Verbs

Reflexive verbs are conjugated with *être* in the *passé composé*. In conformity with the rule just above, the past participle agrees in number and gender with the reflexive pronoun only when it is the <u>direct object</u> (notice the elision of *te* and *se* before vowels): **se lever** (*to get up*): **je me suis levé, je me suis levée; tu t'es levé, tu t'es levée; il s'est levé, elle s'est levée; nous nous sommes levés, nous nous sommes levées; vous vous êtes levé, vous vous êtes levée, vous vous êtes levés, vous vous êtes levées; ils se sont levés, elles se sont levées.**

s'asseoir (*to sit down*): **je me suis assis, je me suis assise; tu t'es assis, tu t'es assise; il s'est assis, elle s'est assise; nous nous sommes assis, nous nous sommes assises; vous vous êtes assis, vous vous êtes assise, vous vous êtes assis, vous vous êtes assises; ils se sont assis, elles se sont assises.**

Agreement is not shown when the reflexive pronoun is used as an indirect complement. The most common of these constructions involve reflexive constructions with parts of the body: **Elle s'est lavée.** (*She washed. She washed herself.*) But: **Elle s'est lavé les mains.** (*She washed her hands.*) **Ils se sont brossés.** (*They brushed [themselves].*) But: **Ils se sont brossé les dents.** (*They brushed their teeth.*)

Remember!

In reflexive constructions with indirect objects, the past participle agrees in number and gender with any other complement preceding the verb: **Ils se sont acheté une nouvelle voiture.** [no agreement] (*They bought themselves a new car.*) **La voiture qu'ils se sont achetée est bleue.** (*The car they bought themselves is blue.*) **Quelle voiture se sont-ils achetée?** (*Which car did they buy for themselves?*)

Use of the *Passé Composé*

The *Passé Composé* as Present Perfect

Historically and formally, the *passé composé* is the present perfect tense. The action or condition expressed by the present perfect is completed, but in the very recent past; or else it was completed in the distant past, but still has bearing on the present. The time of completion is indefinite: **Elle a été très malade.** (*She has been very ill.*) **Sont-ils revenus de Paris?** (*Have they come back from Paris?*) **Ils ont visité Québec deux fois.** (*They have visited Quebec twice.*)

The *Passé Composé* as the Conversational Past

Far more often the passé composé is used—in conversation, informal writing, and literary writing that imitates informal style—as a past tense to express an action or a condition completed or ended at a definite time in the past. It replaces the *passé simple*, which has fallen out of use except in formal writing. It is commonly accompanied by such adverbs and adverbial expressions as the following: **hier** (*yesterday*), **avant-hier** (*the day before yesterday*), **hier soir** (*last evening, last night*), **l'autre jour** (*the other day*), **la semaine dernière** (or **passée**) (*last week*), **l'année passée** (or **dernière**) (*last year*): **Hier nous sommes allés au cinéma.** (*Yesterday we went to the movies.*) **On a bâti cette cathédrale au neuvième siècle.** (*This cathedral was built in the ninth century.*) **Elle s'est couchée de bonne heure hier soir.** (*She went to bed early last night.*) **Christophe Colomb a découvert les Antilles.** (*Christopher Columbus discovered the Antilles.*)

Differences Between the *Passé Composé* and the Imperfect

The imperfect is used to describe continuing, habitual action or a past action or condition of long duration; the *passé composé* implies completion at a definite time in the past. Very often English does not make the distinction: **Il a joué au football hier.** (*He played soccer yesterday.*) **Il jouait au football tous les samedis.** (*He played soccer every Saturday.*) **Elle lui a parlé une fois.** (*She spoke to him once.*) **Elle lui parlait souvent.** (*She often spoke to him.*) **Tu l'as vu l'autre jour.** (*You saw him the other day.*) **Tu le voyais bien des fois.** (*You saw him many* *times.*) **J'y suis allée l'année passée.** (*I went there last year.*) **J'y allais tous les ans.** (*I went there every year.*) The imperfect describes what was going on when a specific event occurred; the event is expressed in the *passé composé*: **Ils dansaient quand nous sommes arrivés.** (*They were dancing when we arrived.*) **Je dînais quand elle est partie.** (*I was having dinner when she left.*) **Il a neigé pendant que nous dormions.** (*It snowed while we were sleeping.*) Sometimes the tense will change depending upon whether the speaker wishes to portray the event as a background condition or as something that happened: **Un homme a vendu la peinture et l'autre l'a achetée.** (*One man sold the painting and the other bought it.*) **Un homme vendait la peinture et l'autre l'achetait quand elle est tombée du cadre.** (*One man was selling the painting and the other was buying it when it fell out of the frame.*)**J'ai eu peur quand le voleur est entré dans la maison.** (*I was frightened [= became afraid] when the thief came into the house.*) **J'avais peur quand le voleur était dans la maison.** (*I was frightened when [= while] the thief was in the house.*)

The *Plus-Que-Parfait* or Pluperfect Tense

Formation of the Pluperfect

The pluperfect is formed by using the imperfect form of the auxiliary verb with the past participle. Rules for the agreement of the past participle of verbs conjugated with *être* and reflexive verbs are the same as for the *passé composé*: **parler** (*to speak*): **j'avais parlé**; **tu avais parlé**; **il, elle, on avait parlé**; **nous avions parlé**; **vous aviez parlé**; **ils, elles avaient parlé**.

venir (*to come*): **j'étais venu(e)**; **tu étais venu(e)**; **il était venu, elle était venue**; **nous étions venu(s)(es)**; **vous étiez venu(e)(s)(es)**; **ils étaient venus, elles étaient venues**.

s'asseoir (*to sit down*): **je m'étais assis(e)**; **tu t'étais assis(e)**; **il s'était assis, elle s'était assise**; **nous nous étions assis(es)**; **vous vous étiez assis(e)(s)(es)**; **ils s'étaient assis, elles s'étaient assises**.

You Need to Know ✔

Uses of the Pluperfect

The pluperfect is used, like the past perfect in English, to express a past action completed before another past action. **Ils avaient déjà terminé quand je suis arrivée.** (*They had already finished when I arrived.*)

It can also be used with the imperfect to express a habitual action that was always completed before another habitual action: **Quand j'avais fini mes devoirs, j'allais jouer avec mes amis.** (*When I had finished my homework, I would go play with my friends.*)

The *Futur Antérieur* or Future Perfect

Formation of the Future Perfect

The future perfect is formed with the future of the auxiliary verb with the past participle. The rules for the agreement of past participles are the same as for the other compound tenses: **parler** (*to speak*): **j'aurai parlé**; tu **auras parlé**; il, elle, on **aura parlé**; nous **aurons parlé**; vous **aurez parlé**; ils, elles **auront parlé**.

venir (*to come*): je **serai venu(e)**; tu **seras venu(e)**; il **sera venu**, elle **sera venue**; nous **serons venu(s)(es)**; vous **serez venu(e)(s)(es)**; ils **seront venus**, elles **seront venues**.

s'asseoir (*to sit down*): je me **serai assis(e)**; tu te **seras assis(e)**; il se **sera assis**, elle se **sera assise**; nous nous **serons assis(es)**; vous vous **serez assis(e)(s)(es)**; ils se **seront assis**, elles se **seront assises**.

Uses of the Future Perfect

The future perfect tense is used to express a future action that will be completed before another action in the future. Notice that in nearly every case French requires the future tense in the dependent clause: **Il sera déjà parti quand vous arriverez.** (*He will have already left* when *you arrive.*) **Nous nous <u>serons couchés</u> quand vous reviendrez.** (*We'<u>ll</u> <u>have gone to bed</u> when you come back.*) **Elles <u>auront mangé</u> avant mon arrivée.** (*They <u>will have eaten</u> before my arrival.*) **Demain à cette heure, nous <u>serons arrivés</u> en France.** (*Tomorrow at this time we'<u>ll</u> <u>have arrived</u> in France.*)

The future perfect is also used after the following conjunctions with the future or future perfect in the main clause. Notice that in nearly every case English uses the present or the present perfect in the dependent clause: **après que** (*after*), **quand** (*when*), **aussitôt que** (*as soon as*), **tant que** (*until*), **dès que** (*as soon as*): **Nous nous coucherons après qu'elle <u>sera partie</u>.** (*We will go to bed after she <u>leaves</u>.*) **Tu me téléphoneras dès que tu <u>auras lu</u> l'histoire.** (*You'll telephone me as soon as you <u>have read</u> the story.*) **Nous dînerons quand ils <u>seront rentrés</u>.** (*We'll have dinner when they <u>have come</u> home.*) **Nous travaillerons tant qu'il aura réussi à l'examen.** (*We shall work until he <u>has passed</u> the examination.*)

Like the future tense, the future perfect is sometimes used to express probability: **Il n'est pas ici. Il <u>sera parti</u>.** (*He is not here. He must have left.*) **Je ne peux pas trouver mon journal. Je l'<u>aurai jeté</u>.** (*I can't find my newspaper. I must have thrown it away.*)

The Past Conditional (*Passé du Conditionnel*)

Formation of the Past Conditional

The past conditional is formed by using the conditional of the auxiliary verb with the past participle. The rules for the agreement of the past participle are the same as for the other compound tenses: **parler** (*to speak*): **j'<u>aurais parlé</u>; tu <u>aurais parlé</u>; il, elle, on <u>aurait parlé</u>; nous <u>aurions</u> <u>parlé</u>; vous <u>auriez parlé</u>; ils, elles <u>auraient parlé</u>.**

venir (*to come*): **je <u>serais venu(e)</u>; tu <u>serais venu(e)</u>; il <u>serait</u> <u>venu</u>, elle <u>serait venue</u>; nous <u>serions venu(s)(es)</u>; vous <u>seriez</u> <u>venu(e)(s) (es)</u>; ils <u>seraient venus</u>, elles <u>seraient venues</u>.**

s'asseoir (*to sit down*): **je me <u>serais assis(e)</u>; tu te <u>serais assis(e)</u>; il se <u>serait assis</u>, elle se <u>serait assise</u>; nous nous <u>serions assis(es)</u>; vous vous <u>seriez assis(e)(s)(es)</u>; ils se <u>seraient assis</u>, elles se <u>seraient</u> <u>assises</u>.**

Use of the Past Conditional

The past conditional is used to describe what would have taken place if something else had not interfered: **Ils <u>auraient fait</u> le voyage, mais ils n'avaient pas assez d'argent.** (*They would have made the trip, but they did not have enough money.*) **Elle <u>serait venue</u>, mais elle n'avait pas d'auto.** (*She would have come, but she didn't have a car.*) **Dans ce cas-là, j'<u>aurais refusé</u>.** (*In that case, I would have refused.*)

The past conditional may also be used to express a possible action in the past: **J'ai trouvé sa note. <u>Serait-il venu</u> en mon absence?** (*I found his note. <u>Could he have come</u> in my absence?*)

The past conditional is also used to describe an action that is unsure. Like the parallel construction in the present conditional, it is typical of journalistic style: **Dix avions <u>auraient été</u> abbatus hier.** (<u>*It is reported that*</u> *ten planes* <u>*were brought down*</u> *yesterday.*)

The *Passé Antérieur* or Past Anterior

Like the *passé simple*, the *passé antérieur* is a literary tense that is not used in conversation or in informal writing.

Formation of the *Passé Antérieur*

The *passé antérieur* is formed by the *passé simple* of the auxiliary with the past participle. The rules for agreement of past participles are the same as for the other compound tenses: **parler** (*to speak*): **j'<u>eus parlé</u>**; **tu <u>eus parlé</u>**; **il, elle, on <u>eut parlé</u>**; **nous <u>eûmes parlé</u>**; **vous <u>eûtes parlé</u>**; **ils, elles <u>eurent parlé</u>**.

venir (*to come*): **je <u>fus venu(e)</u>**; **tu <u>fus venu(e)</u>**; **il <u>fut venu</u>**, **elle <u>fut venue</u>**; **nous <u>fûmes venu(s)(es)</u>**; **vous <u>fûtes venu(e)(s)(es)</u>**; **ils <u>furent venus</u>**; **elles <u>furent venues</u>**.

s'asseoir (*to sit down*): **je me fus assis(e)**; **tu te fus assis(e)**; **il se fut assis, elle se fut assise**; **nous nous fûmes assis(es)**; **vous vous fûtes assis(e)(s)(es)**; **ils se furent assis, elles se furent assises.**

Use of the *Passé Antérieur*

In formal written style it is used to express a past action preceding another past action; when the *passé antérieur* is used, the latter is expressed in the *passé simple*: **Quand il eut fini, il partit.** (*When he had finished, he left.*) **Lorsqu'elle fut arrivée, nous partîmes.** (*When she had arrived, we left.*) **Quand elles se furent réunies, elles élurent une présidente.** (*When they had gathered, they elected a president.*) **Après qu'ils eurent élu un représentant, ils retournèrent au travail.** (*After they had elected a representative, they went back to work.*) **Aussitôt qu'elle eut appris la nouvelle, elle décida de partir.** (*As soon as she learned the news, she decided to leave.*)

Si Clauses

Si (*if*) clauses are used to express conditions. For such clauses, there is a definite sequence of tenses to be followed.

Conditions based in fact or possible fact:

Si clause	Result clause
present indicative	future or imperative
passé composé	future or imperative

Conditions contrary to fact:

Si clause	Result clause
imperfect	present conditional
pluperfect	past conditional

General rules:

Si clause	Result clause
present indicative	present indicative

The imperfect-present conditional sequence is used in reference to present time; the pluperfect-past conditional sequence refers to past time. English uses the subjunctive in conditions contrary to fact; in French, except in very formal writing, when the imperfect and pluperfect subjunctive may be used (see below), the indicative is used. Notice that *si* becomes *s'* before *il* and *ils*, but it does <u>not</u> elide before *on* or *elle(s)*: **Si elle <u>a</u> assez d'argent, elle <u>fera</u> le voyage.** (*If she <u>has</u> enough money, she <u>will take</u> the trip.* Perhaps she will have the money.) **Si vous <u>n'avez pas compris</u>, <u>dites</u>-le-moi.** (*If you <u>haven't understood</u>, <u>tell</u> me.* Perhaps you did understand.) **Si vous <u>n'avez pas compris</u>, vous me le <u>direz</u>.** (*If you have not understood, you will tell me.* Perhaps you did understand.) **S'il <u>avait</u> l'argent, il <u>ferait</u> le voyage.** (*If he <u>had</u> the money, he <u>would take</u> the trip.* But he does not have the money.) **Si j'étais président, je <u>ne signerais pas</u> ce traité.** (*If I <u>were</u> president, I <u>would not sign</u> this treaty.* But I am not president.) **Si j'avais eu l'argent, j'<u>aurais fait</u> le voyage.** (*If I had had the money, I would have taken the trip.* I did not have the money and I did not take the trip.) **Si on <u>étudie</u>, on <u>reçoit</u> de bonnes notes.** (*If you <u>study</u>, you <u>get</u> good grades.*) **Si j'<u>ai</u> faim, je <u>mange</u>.** (*If I <u>am</u> hungry, I <u>eat</u>.*)

The Subjunctive Mood

The indicative mood is used to imply truth, fact, or probability. It reports an action as actually taking place (present) or having taken place (imperfect, *passé composé*, etc.) or as probable or certain to take place (future): **Marie <u>rougit</u> souvent.** (*Marie <u>blushes</u> a lot.*) **Je sais qu'il <u>est sorti</u>.** (*I know that he <u>went out</u>.*) **Il est probable qu'il <u>ira</u> à Paris.** (*It is probable that he<u>'ll go</u> to Paris.*) **Il est vrai que la terre <u>est</u> ronde.** (*It is true that the earth <u>is</u> round.*)

The subjunctive mood expresses an action or an idea that is subordinated to an emotional perspective, a personal desire, the will of an individual, or an internal or external necessity. Or else the idea in the dependent clause is contrary to fact, doubtful, or merely possible, but not probable: **Il veut qu'<u>elle devienne</u> médecin.** (*He wants <u>her to become</u> a doctor.*) **Il faut qu'<u>elle se réveille</u> tôt.** (*It is necessary <u>for her to wake up</u> early.*) **Je doute qu'il <u>vienne</u> demain.** (*I doubt that he <u>will come</u> tomorrow.*) **Elle regrette qu'il <u>soit</u> malade.** (*She is sorry that he <u>is</u> ill.*)

In the first example, she is not yet a doctor and she may never be; the possibility is less significant than his desire. In the second and third examples, her waking up early and his coming tomorrow are also not actual events. In the last example, one person's illness is presented in terms of another person's emotional response to the illness.

Notice also that in the last two examples English structure parallels the French—a main clause followed by a subordinate clause, although English uses the indicative. In the first two examples, English uses an infinitive structure, while French requires a subordinate clause.

The Present Subjunctive

Formation of the Present Subjunctive

Endings

With the exception of only two verbs (*avoir* and *être*), the present subjunctive is formed by adding the following endings to a subjunctive stem:

	singular	plural
1st	**-e**	**-ions**
2nd	**-es**	**-iez**
3rd	**-e**	**-ent**

Note that the 1st, 2nd and 3rd singular and 3rd plural endings are identical with the Set 1 present indicative endings, while 1st and 2nd plural endings resemble the corresponding persons in the imperfect.

Subjunctive Stems: Regular Derivations

The present subjunctive is conjugated following a pattern of one or two stems. In the case of a two-stem subjunctive, one stem serves the singular forms and the 3rd plural and the other the 1st and 2nd plural; this is a familiar pattern in French verbs pointed out many times before.

To find the subjunctive stem or stems, the 1st and the 3rd plural forms of the present indicative are compared and the endings -*ons* and -*ent* are removed. If the remaining stems are identical, the present subjunctive has one stem; if the remaining stems are different, the present subjunctive has two stems.

First, Second, and Third Conjugations

First Conjugation verbs (except those involving spelling changes) as well as Second and Third Conjugation verbs and related verbs have one stem: **parler** (*to speak*) <u>parlons</u> / <u>parlent</u>: je parl<u>e</u>; tu parl<u>es</u>; il, elle, on parl<u>e</u>; nous parl<u>ions</u>; vous parl<u>iez</u>; ils, elles parl<u>ent</u>b.

finir (*to finish*) <u>finissons</u> / <u>finissent</u>: je finiss<u>e</u>; tu finiss<u>es</u>; il, elle, on finiss<u>e</u>; nous finiss<u>ions</u>; vous finiss<u>iez</u>; ils, elles finiss<u>ent</u>.

répondre (*to answer*) <u>répondons</u> / <u>répondent</u>: je répond<u>e</u>; tu répond<u>es</u>; il, elle, on répond<u>e</u>; nous répond<u>ions</u>; vous répond<u>iez</u>; ils, elles répond<u>ent</u>.

dormir (*to sleep*) <u>dormons</u> / <u>dorment</u>: je dorm<u>e</u>; tu dorm<u>es</u>; il, elle, on dorm<u>e</u>; nous dorm<u>ions</u>; vous dorm<u>iez</u>; ils, elles dorm<u>ent</u>.

rompre (*to break*) <u>rompons</u> / <u>rompent</u>: je romp<u>e</u>; tu romp<u>es</u>; il, elle, on romp<u>e</u>; nous romp<u>ions</u>; vous romp<u>iez</u>; ils, elles romp<u>ent</u>.

mettre (*to put*) <u>mettons</u> / <u>mettent</u>: je mett<u>e</u>; tu mett<u>es</u>; il, elle, on mett<u>e</u>; nous mett<u>ions</u>; vous mett<u>iez</u>; ils, elles mett<u>ent</u>.

Verbs with Infinitives Ending in -cer and -ger

These verbs do <u>not</u> require spelling changes (see above): **avancer: nous avançons** (indicative), **nous avancions** (subj.); **manger: nous mangeons** (indicative), **nous mangions** (subj.).

Verbs with -é- as the Last Vowel in the Stem

These verbs have two stems:
compléter (*to complete*) <u>complétons</u> / <u>complètent</u>: je <u>complète</u>; tu <u>complètes</u>; il, elle, on <u>complète</u>; nous <u>complét</u>ions; vous <u>complét</u>iez; ils, elles <u>complètent</u>.

Verbs with "Mute e" as the Last Vowel in the Stem

These verbs have two stems: **lever** (*to raise*) <u>levons</u> / <u>lèvent</u>: je <u>lève</u>; tu <u>lèves</u>; il, elle, on <u>lève</u>; nous <u>lev</u>ions; vous <u>lev</u>iez; ils, elles <u>lèvent</u>.

jeter (*to throw*) <u>jetons</u> / <u>jettent</u>: je <u>jette</u>; tu <u>jettes</u>; il, elle, on <u>jette</u>; nous <u>jet</u>ions; vous <u>jet</u>iez; ils, elles <u>jettent</u>.

Verbs with –y- as the Last Letter in the Stem

These verbs have two stems: **payer** (*to pay, pay for*) **pay~~ons~~ / pai~~ent~~**: je **paie**; tu **paies**; il, elle, on **paie**; nous **payions**; vous **payiez**; ils, elles **paient.**

Irregular Verbs with One Stem

Most irregular verbs have one stem: **ouvrir(ouvr~~ons~~/ouvr~~ent~~)**: j'**ouvre**, nous **ouvrions**; courir (**cour~~ons~~/ cour~~ent~~**): je **coure**, nous **courions**; connaître (**connaiss~~ons~~/ connaiss~~ent~~**): je **connaisse**, nous **connaissions**; plaire (**plais~~ons~~/plais~~ent~~**): je **plaise**, nous **plaisions**; lire (**lis~~ons~~/lis~~ent~~**): je **lise**, nous **lisions**; dire (**dis~~ons~~/dis~~ent~~**): je **dise**, nous **disions**; conduire (**conduis~~ons~~/conduis~~ent~~**): je **conduise**, nous **conduisions**; suivre (**suiv~~ons~~/suiv~~ent~~**): je **suive**, nous **suivions**; craindre (**craign~~ons~~/ craign~~ent~~**): je **craigne**, nous **craignions**; s'asseoir (**assey~~ons~~/ assey~~ent~~**): je m'**asseye**, nous nous **asseyions**.

Irregular Verbs with Two Stems

venir (*to come*) **ven~~ons~~ / vienn~~ent~~**: je **vienne**; tu **viennes**; il, elle, on **vienne**; nous **venions**; vous **veniez**; ils, elles **viennent**;

Also: **tenir** (**ten~~ons~~/tienn~~ent~~**): je **tienne**, nous **tenions**; prendre (**pren~~ons~~/ prenn~~ent~~**): je **prenne**, nous **prenions**; mourir (**mour~~ons~~/ meur~~ent~~**): je **meure**, nous **mourions**; boire (**buv~~ons~~/boiv~~ent~~**): je **boive**, nous **buvions**; devoir (**dev~~ons~~/doiv~~ent~~**): je **doive**, nous **devions**; recevoir (**recev~~ons~~/ reçoiv~~ent~~**): je **reçoive**, nous **recevions**; voir (**voy~~ons~~/ voi~~ent~~**): je **voie**, nous **voyions**; croire (**croy~~ons~~/ croi~~ent~~**): je **croie**, nous **croyions**; (pleuvoir: il **pleuve**).

Subjunctive Stems: Irregular Derivations

Verbs with One Subjunctive Stem

Three verbs with one-stem subjunctives are irregular (notice, however, that the endings are regular): **pouvoir** (*to be able*): je **puisse**; tu **puisses**; il, elle, on **puisse**; nous **puissions**; vous **puissiez**; ils, elles **puissent**; **faire** (*to do, to make*): je **fasse**; tu **fasses**; il, elle, on **fasse**; nous **fassions**; vous **fassiez**; ils, elles **fassent**.

savoir (*to know*): je sache; tu saches; il, elle, on sache; nous sachions; vous sachiez; ils, elles sachent.

Verbs with Two Subjunctive Stems

Three verbs have one irregular and one regular stem: **aller** (*to go*): **j'aille; tu ailles; il, elle, on aille; nous allions** (cf. nous allons); **vous alliez; ils, elles aillent.**

valoir (*to be worth*): **je vaille; tu vailles; il, elle, on vaille; nous valions** (cf. nous valons); **vous valiez; ils, elles vaillent.**

vouloir (*to wish, to want*): **je veuille; tu veuilles; il, elle, on veuille; nous voulions** (cf. nous voulons); **vous vouliez; ils, elles veuillent. Falloir** (*to be necessary*) is in this class: **il faille.**

Verbs with Irregular Subjunctives

Avoir and *être* have irregular subjunctives:
avoir (*to have*): **j'aie; tu aies; il, elle, on ait; nous ayons; vous ayez; ils, elles aient.**

être (*to be*): **je sois; tu sois; il, elle, on soit; nous soyons; vous soyez; ils, elles soient.**

Uses of the Present Subjunctive

In Noun Clauses

The subjunctive is required in subordinate clauses following verbs and verbal expressions denoting desire, doubt, denial, necessity, and fear. Such clauses are invariably introduced with the conjunction *que*. Although *that* is often omitted in English, *que* is never dropped in French. Some common expressions requiring the subjunctive are:

* Wish, preference, or desire: **aimer mieux** (*to prefer*), **désirer** (*to desire*), **préférer** (*to prefer*), **souhaiter** (*to wish*), **vouloir** (*to wish, to want*), **bien voluoir** (*to agree, to be willing*): **Je veux qu'il parte.** (*I want him to leave.*) **Je veux bien qu'il aille avec nous.** (*I am willing for him to go with us.*) **Je souhaite que tu réussisses.** (*I wish you to succeed.*) **Je préfère qu'il rentre à midi.** (*I prefer that he come back at noon.*)

Note that *espérer* (*to hope*) always takes the indicative in French: **J'espère qu'il ira bientôt mieux.** (*I hope that he will get better soon.*)

- Doubt and denial: **douter** (*to doubt*), **ne pas croire** (*not to believe*), **ne pas penser** (*not to think*), **nier** (*to deny*): **Je doute qu'il vienne.** (*I doubt that he will come.*) **Elle nie qu'elle te connaisse.** (*She denies that she knows you.*) **Je ne crois pas que ce soit vrai.** (*I don't believe that it is true.*) **Il ne pense pas que je sois ici.** (*He doesn't think that I am here.*) Note that *croire* and *penser* in the affirmative require the indicative: **Je crois que c'est vrai.** (*I believe that it is true.*) **Il pense que je suis à Montréal.** (*He thinks that I am in Montreal.*)

- Emotions and feelings: **être content** (*to be happy*), **être heureux** (*to be happy*), **être triste** (*to be sad*), **être fâché** (*to be angry*), **être furieux** (*to be furious*), **être fier** (*to be proud*), **être désolé** (*to be sorry*), **être surpris** (*to be surprised*), **avoir peur** (*to be afraid*), **avoir crainte** (*to be afraid*), **craindre** (*to fear*), **regretter** (*to regret*), **se fâcher** (*to get angry*), **se réjouir** (*to rejoice*): **Elle est heureuse que vous puissiez venir.** (*She is happy that you can come.*) **Nous sommes tristes que vous partiez.** (*We are sad that you are leaving.*) **Elle craint que nous n'attendions pas.** (*She is afraid that we won't wait.*)

- Command, requirement, request: **commander** (*to ask, order*), **demander** (*to ask, request*), **exiger** (*to demand, require*), **ordonner** (*to command*): **Il exige que nous soyons à l'heure.** (*He requires us to be on time.*) **Il demande que je vienne le voir.** (*He asks me to come see him.*) **Le médecin ordonne que tu boives trois verres d'eau par jour.** (*The doctor orders you to drink three glasses of water a day.*)

- Permission, refusal of permission: **consentir** (*to consent*), **défendre** (*to forbid*), **empêcher** (*to prevent*), **interdire** (*to forbid*), **permettre** (*to permit*): **Il permet que nous fassions cela.** (*He permits us to do that.*) **Il interdit que nous sortions.** (*He forbids us to go out.*) **Je consens que tu partes.** (*I consent to your leaving.*)

Impersonal Expressions of Opinion, Emotion, and Doubt

Common impersonal expressions requiring the subjunctive include the following:

- Opinion: **il est temps** (*it is time*), **il est grand temps** (*it is high time*), **il vaut mieux que** (*it is better*), **il est préférable** (*it is preferable*), **il faut** (*it is necessary*), **il est nécessaire** (*it is necessary*), **il est essentiel** (*it is essential*), **il importe** (*it is important*), **il est important** (*it is important*), **il suffit** (*it suffices, it is enough*), **il est indispensable** (*it is indispensable*), **il est naturel** (*it is natural*), **il convient que** (*it is fitting, it is proper*), **il est convenable** (*it is fitting, it is proper*), **il est possible** (*it is possible*), **il se peut** (*it is possible*), **il est impossible** (*it is impossible*), **il est utile** (*it is useful*), **il est inutile** (*it is useless*), **il est urgent** (*it is urgent*): <u>Il est temps que vous veniez.</u> (*It is time <u>that you came</u>.*) <u>Il faut que vous étudiez.</u> (*It is necessary <u>that you study</u>.*) <u>Il est essential que nous recevions</u> ces lettres. (*It is essential <u>that we receive</u> those letters.*) <u>Il suffit que tu le dises.</u> (*It is enough <u>that you say it</u>.*) <u>Il est possible qu'elle mente.</u> (*It is possible <u>that she is lying</u>.*) <u>Il est naturel que vous pleuriez.</u> (*It is natural <u>for you to cry</u>.*)
- Emotion: **il est heureux** (*it is fortunate*), **il est bon** (*it is good*), **c'est dommage** (*it is a pity, it's too bad*), **il est dommage** (*it is a pity, it's too bad*), **il est honteux** (*it is shameful*), **il est triste** (*it is sad*), **il est surprenant** (*it is surprising*), **il est étonnant** (*it is astonishing*): <u>C'est dommage qu'elle ne vienne pas.</u> (*It's a pity <u>that she's not coming</u>.*) <u>Il est honteux qu'il dise cela.</u> (*It is a shame <u>that he says that</u>.*)
- Doubt: **il est douteux** (*it is doubtful*), **il est peu probable** (*it is improbable, unlikely*), **il n'est pas certain** (*it is uncertain*), **il n'est pas sûr** (*it is not sure*), **il est impensable** (*it is unthinkable*): <u>Il est douteux qu'il réussisse.</u> (*It is doubtful <u>that he will succeed</u>.*) <u>Il est peu probable qu'il pleuve.</u> (*It is unlikely <u>that it will rain</u>.*)

The Subjunctive Versus the Indicative in Expressions of Certainty and Doubt

Many of the expressions above take the indicative when they are affirmative and the subjunctive when they are negative or in the interrogative. The future as well as the present occurs in the indicative. **Il est sûr <u>qu'il viendra</u>.** But: **Il n'est pas sûr <u>qu'il vienne</u>. Est-il sûr <u>qu'il vienne</u>? Il est certain <u>qu'elle comprend</u>.** But: **Il n'est pas certain <u>qu'elle comprenne</u>. Est-il certain**

qu'elle comprenne? Je pense **qu'il vient.** But: **Je ne pense pas qu'il vienne. Penses-tu qu'il vienne?** Je crois **qu'elle comprend.** But: **Je ne crois pas qu'elle comprenne. Penses-tu qu'elle comprenne?**

The Subjunctive with Subordinating Conjunctions

Many conjunctions require the subjunctive:

- Of time: **avant que** (*before*), **jusqu'à ce que** (*until*): **Nous joue- rons jusqu'à ce qu'il fasse nuit.** (*We will play until it gets dark.*) In writing, *avant que* often takes expletive *ne*: **On lui dira au revoir avant qu'il ne parte.** (*We will tell him good-bye before he leaves.*)
- Of cause or negation: **non que, non pas que** (*not that*), **sans que** (*without*): **Je l'adore de tout cœur—non pas qu'elle soit parfaite.** (*I love her with my whole heart—not that she is perfect.*) **Elle est partie sans que je la voie.** (*She left without my seeing her.*)
- Of purpose or result: **afin que** (*so that, in order that*), **pour que** (*so that, in order that*), **de façon que** (*so that, in such a way that*), **de manière que** (*so that, in such a way that*), **de crainte que** (*for fear that*), **de peur que** (*for fear that*): **Je dis ceci afin que tu com- prennes.** (*I'm saying this so that you will understand.*) **Il parle de manière qu'elle puisse le comprendre.** (*He speaks in such a way that she can understand him.*)
- In writing and careful speech expressions of fear require expletive *ne*: **Elle se tait de peur que vous ne la réprimandiez.** (*She keeps quiet for fear that you will scold her.*)
- Of concession: **bien que** (*although*), **quoique** (*although*), **encore que** (*although*), **malgré que** (*despite the fact that*): **Bien qu'il soit chez lui, il ne répond pas à la téléphone.** (*Although he is at home, he does not answer the telephone.*) **Malgré qu'il ait cinquante ans, on le croirait lycéen.** (*Despite the fact that he is fifty, you'd think he was a high school boy.*)
- Of condition: **à condition que** (*on the condition that*), **pourvu que** (*provided that*), **supposé que** (*supposing that*), **à moins que** (*unless*), **soit que . . . soit que** (*whether . . . or*): **Je vous attendrai à condition que vous arriviez avant six heures.** (*I will wait for you on condition that you arrive before six o'clock.*) **Soit qu'il vive, soit qu'il meure, il n'abandonnera pas son poste.** (*Whether he lives or dies, he will not abandon his post.*)

- In writing and in careful speech, *à moins que* requires expletive *ne*: **Ils iront à la plage à moins qu'il ne pleuve.** (*They will go to the beach unless it rains*.)

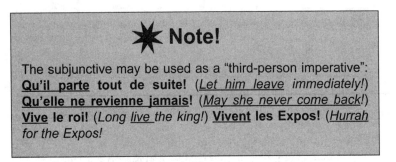

✴ Note!

The subjunctive may be used as a "third-person imperative":
Qu'il parte tout de suite! (*Let him leave immediately!*)
Qu'elle ne revienne jamais! (*May she never come back!*)
Vive le roi! (*Long live the king!*) **Vivent les Expos!** (*Hurrah for the Expos!*

The Subjunctive in Relative Clauses

- Indefinite Antecedent. The subjunctive is used in relative clauses when the antecedent (the word the clause modifies) is indefinite—that is, when the relative pronoun indentifies someone or something not yet found or identified. If the antecedent is definite, the indicative is used: **Je connais un médecin qui peut m'aider.** [definite] (*I know a doctor who can help me*.) **Je cherche un médecin qui puisse m'aider.** [indefinite] (*I'm looking for a doctor who can help me*.) **Y a-t-il quelqu'un qui sache parler français?** (*Is there someone who can speak French?*)
- After *rien* (*nothing*) and *personne* (*no one*): The subjunctive is used in relative clauses modifying *rien* and *personne* because they are indefinite: **Il n'y a rien qui lui plaise.** (*There's nothing that pleases him*.) **Il n'y a personne que vous puissiez tolérer.** (*There is no one whom you can tolerate*.)
- With the superlative and with *seul* (*only*): The subjunctive is used in relative clauses modifying a superlative and with *seul* when they imply absolute exclusivity: **C'est le plus beau poème que je connaisse.** (*This is the most beautiful poem I know*.) **C'est la seule femme qu'il puisse aimer.** (*She is the only woman whom he can love*.)

The Subjunctive with Indefinite Adjectives and Adverbs

The following adverbial expressions require the subjunctive: **si . . . que** (*however . . .*), **quelque . . .** (*however . . .* [invariable]), **quelque . . . que** (*whatever*), **quel que** (*whatever*), **où que** (*wherever*): <u>Si intelligente qu'elle soit</u>, elle ne pourra pas comprendre. (*<u>However intelligent she may be,</u> she won't be able to understand.*) <u>Quelque forts que vous soyez</u>, vous ne pourrez pas le faire. (*<u>However strong you may be,</u> you will not be able to do it.*) <u>Quelques fautes que les étudiants fassent</u>, il faut les encourager. (*<u>Whatever mistakes the students may make,</u> you must encourage them.*) <u>Quelques soient vos problèmes</u>, vous pourrez les résoudre. (*<u>Whatever your problems are,</u> you'll be able to resolve them.*) Je vous suivrai <u>où que vous alliez</u>. (*I'll follow you <u>wherever you go</u>.*)

The Subjunctive with Indefinite Pronouns

The following indefinite pronouns require the subjunctive: **qui que** (*whoever, whomever*), **quoi que** (*whatever*): <u>Qui que vous soyez</u>, vous n'avez pas le droit de m'insulter. (*<u>Whoever you are,</u> you don't have the right to insult me.*) <u>Quoi que tu dises</u>, je te croirai. (*<u>Whatever you say</u>, I'll believe you.*)

The Past Subjunctive

Formation of the Past Subjunctive

The past subjunctive is the subjunctive of the *passé composé*. It is formed by using the present subjunctive of the auxiliary with the past participle. The rules for agreement of past participles are the same as for the other compound tenses: **parler** (*to speak*): j'<u>aie parlé</u>; tu <u>ais parlé</u>; il, elle, on <u>ait parlé</u>; nous <u>ayons parlé</u>; vous <u>ayez parlé</u>; ils, elles <u>aient parlé</u>; venir (*to come*): je sois <u>venu(e)</u>; tu <u>sois venu(e)</u>; il <u>soit venu</u>, elle <u>soit venue</u>; nous <u>soyons venu(s)(es)</u>; vous <u>soyez venu(e)(s)(es)</u>; ils <u>soient venus</u>, elles <u>soient venues</u>.

   s'asseoir (*to sit down*): je me <u>sois assis(e)</u>; tu te sois <u>assis(e)</u>; il se <u>soit assis</u>, elle se <u>soit assise</u>; nous nous <u>soyons assis(es)</u>; vous vous <u>soyez assis(e)(s)(es)</u>; ils se <u>soient assis</u>, elles se <u>soient assises</u>.

You Need to Know ✔

Use of the Past Subjunctive

The past subjunctive is used in subordinate clauses referring to past time. In the subjunctive, no distinction is made in speech and in informal writing between completed and uncompleted actions or conditions:
Je regrette <u>qu'il n'ait pas attendu</u>. (*I regret <u>that he did not wait</u>*.) **Je suis content <u>qu'elle soit venue</u>.** (*I am glad <u>that she came</u>*.) **<u>Quoiqu'il ait été malade</u>, il est venu me voir.** (<u>*Although he was ill*</u>, *he came to see me*.)

The Literary Imperfect Subjunctive

Formation

The imperfect subjunctive is formed by adding the following endings to the stem and "theme vowel" used to form the *passé simple*. The endings are the same for all verbs.

	singular	plural
1st	**-sse**	**-ssions**
2nd	**-sses**	**-ssiez**
3rd	**^-t**	**-ssent**

Note that, except for the 3rd singular, the ending following the *-ss-* infix are the same as for the present subjunctive. In the 3rd singular, the "theme vowel" receives a circumflex accent: **parler** (*to speak*): **je par-lasse; tu parl<u>asses</u>; il, elle, on parl<u>ât</u>; nous parl<u>assions</u>; vous parl<u>assiez</u>; ils, elles parl<u>assent</u>**.

aller (*to go*): **j'all<u>asse</u>; tu all<u>asses</u>; il, elle, on all<u>ât</u>; nous all<u>assions</u>; vous all<u>assiez</u>; ils, elles all<u>assent</u>**.

In the Second and Third Conjugation and most related verbs, the "theme vowel" *i* is added to the stem before the basic endings:

Second Conjugation and related verbs: **finir: je finisse, tu finisses, il finît, nous finissions, vous finissiez, ils finissent; haïr: je haïsse,** etc. **dormir: je dormisse,** etc.

Third Conjugation and related verbs: **attendre: j'attendisse, tu attendisses, il attendît, nous attendissions, vous attendissiez, ils attendissent; battre: je battisse,** etc.; **vaincre: je vainquisse,** etc. Notice the spelling change in *vaincre* to indicate that the final consonant in the stem is pronounced *k* rather than *s*. Notice also that in *haïr* the circumflex accent does not replace the dieresis in the 3rd singular.

As in the *passé simple, conclure* and *inclure* maintain *u* as the "theme vowel": **je conclusse, tu conclusses, il conclût,** etc.

Irregular Verbs

- Past participles ending in -i: **rire,** past participle: **ri > je risse,** etc.
- Past participles ending in -u: **connaître,** past participle: **connu > je connusse,** etc.
- Past participles ending in -is: **mettre,** past participle: **mis > je misse,** etc.
- Past participles ending in -it: **dire,** past participle: **dit > je disse,** etc.
- Past participles ending in -uit: **cuire,** past participle: **cuit > je cuisisse,** etc.
- Past participles ending in –int: **craindre,** past participle: **craint > je craignisse,** etc.
- Past participles ending in -ert: **ouvrir,** past participle: **ouvert > j'ouvrisse,** etc.

Other Irregular Verbs

écrire: j'écrivisse, etc.; **voir: je visse,** etc.; **être: je fusse,** etc.; **faire: je fisse,** etc.; **mourir: je mourusse,** etc.; **naître: je naquisse,** etc.; **venir: je vinsse,** etc.

Use of the Imperfect Subjunctive

Like the *passé simple,* the imperfect subjunctive is used only in formal written language. In conversation and in informal writing, the present and past subjunctives have taken over its functions.

In formal writing the imperfect subjunctive is used in subordinate clauses whenever the verb in the main clause is in a past tense: **Je voulais qu'il vînt me voir.** (*I wanted him to come see me.*) **J'étais heureux qu'elles fussent à l'heure.** (*I was happy that they were on time.*) **Elle était trop fatiguée pour que la soirée fût agréable.** (*She was too tired for the evening to be pleasant.*) **Je craignis que l'équipe ne gagnât pas le prix.** (*I was afraid that the team would not win the award.*)

In formal writing the imperfect subjunctive is used in reference to the past when the verb in the main clause is in the present tense: **Je ne crois pas que ce fût comme tu dis.** (*I do not believe that it was as you say.*)

The Literary Pluperfect Subjunctive

Formation

The pluperfect subjunctive is formed by using the imperfect subjunctive of the auxiliary verb with the past participle. The rules for agreement of past participles are the same as for the other compound tenses: **parler** (*to speak*): **j'eusse parlé**; **tu eusses parlé**; **il, elle, on eût parlé**; **nous eussions parlé**; **vous eussiez parlé**; **ils, elles eussent parlé**.

venir (*to come*): **je fusse venu(e)**; **tu fusses venu(e)**; **il fût venu**, **elle fût venue**; **nous fussions venu(s)(es)**; **vous fussiez venu(e)(s)(es)**; **ils fussent venus**, **elles fussent venues**.

s'asseoir (*to sit down*): **je me fusse assis(e)**; **tu te fusses assis(e)**; **il se fût assis**, **elle se fût assise**; **nous nous fussions assis(es)**; **vous vous fussiez assis(e)(s)(es)**; **ils se fussent assis**, **elles se fussent assises**.

Use of the Pluperfect Subjunctive

In formal writing, the pluperfect subjunctive is used to express an action or a condition preceding another action or condition in the past. In conversation and informal writing, the past subjunctive has replaced the pluperfect subjunctive: **Il regrettait que nous ne fussions pas venus.** (*He was sorry that we had not come.*) **Bien qu'il eût déjà mangé, il alla au restaurant quand même.** (*Although he had already eaten, he went to the restaurant just the same.*)

In *si*-clause constructions, the pluperfect subjunctive may be used instead of both the pluperfect indicative and the past conditional: **S'il l'avait cru, il fût parti/S'il l'eût cru, il serait parti/S'il l'eût cru, il fût parti.** (*If he had believed him, he would have left.*)

Uses of the Infinitive

After Prepositions

With two exceptions, the infinitive is the verb form used after prepositions and prepositional expressions: **avant de partir** (*before leaving*), **afin de venir** (*in order to come*), **pour aller** (*in order to go*), **sans voir** (*without seeing*).

En (*while, upon*) is used with the present participle: **en parlant** (*while speaking*), **en partant** (*upon leaving*): **En sortant il nous a dit au revoir.** (*Upon leaving, he told us good-bye.*) **Il s'est endormi en conduisant.** (*He went to sleep while driving.*)

Après is used with the past infinitive, which is formed with the infinitive of the auxiliary and the past participle. In verbs conjugated with *être* the past participle in number and gender with the agent to which it refers; in reflexive verbs, also conjugated with *être*, the participle naturally agrees with the direct object reflexive pronoun: **Après avoir parlé, il est parti.** (*After speaking, he left.*) **Elles sont sorties après s'être habillées.** (*They went out after getting dressed.*) **Ils ont couru dans la maison juste après y être arrivés.** (*They ran into the house right after arriving there.*)

As a Noun

The infinitive is the verb form used as a noun especially with *être*: **Voter est un droit.** (*Voting is a right.*)

When an infinitive complements an infinitive, *c'est* is used in the affirmative, but *ce* is omitted in the negative: **Vouloir c'est pouvoir.** (*To want is to be able to.*) **Vouloir n'est pas avoir.** (*To want is not to have.*)

As an Imperative

In written instructions, the infinitive is used instead of the imperative: **Ne pas marcher sur le gazon.** (*Do not walk on the grass.*) **Entrer sans**

frapper. (_Enter_ *without knocking.*) <u>Laisser cuire</u> **pendant une heure.** (_Cook_ *for one hour.*)

In Fixed Interrogative Phrases Expressing Deliberation

Que <u>faire</u>**?** (*What* <u>shall I [we] do</u>*?*) **Où** <u>aller</u>**?** (*Where* <u>shall I [we] go</u>*?*) **Comment** <u>expliquer</u>**?** (*How* <u>can I [we] explain</u>*?*)

Causative *faire* (the *faire faire* Construction)

An important use of the verb *faire* is in the causative construction where a form of the verb *faire* is used with an infinitive. The subject of *faire* is regarded as causing the action expressed by the infinitive: **Le sucre** <u>fait</u> <u>grossir</u>. (*Sugar* <u>makes you get fat</u>.)

The infinitive may have a subject or a direct object: **Je** <u>fais chanter</u> **les enfants.** (*I* <u>make</u> *the children* <u>sing</u>.) **J'ai fait réciter les élèves.** (*I* <u>made</u> *the students* <u>recite</u>.) **Il** <u>fait laver</u> **la voiture.** (*He* <u>is having</u> *the car* <u>washed</u>.) **Ils** <u>font construire</u> **une maison.** (*They are having a house built.*)

In the first two examples, *les enfants* and *les élèves* are the subjects of the infinitives (the children are singing, the students are reciting). In the last two examples, where in English the construction is passive, *la voiture* and *une maison* are the objects of the infinitives (the work is being done, a house is being built). Notice that in French the word order is the same in both cases.

The infinitive may have both a subject and a direct object. The subject of the infinitive is expressed as an indirect complement, so it is introduced by the preposition *à*; as a noun, it follows the direct object: **Il** <u>fait laver</u> **sa voiture** <u>à son fils</u>. (*He is* <u>having his son wash</u> *his car.*) <u>Fais-tu faire</u> **les dessins** <u>à un architecte</u>**?** (*Are you having* <u>an architect</u> <u>draw</u> *the plans?*)

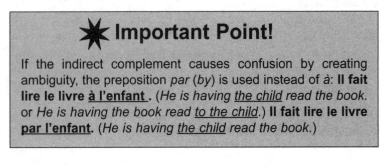

✸ Important Point!

If the indirect complement causes confusion by creating ambiguity, the preposition *par* (*by*) is used instead of *à*: **Il fait lire le livre à l'enfant .** (*He is having* <u>the child</u> *read the book.* or *He is having the book read* <u>to the child</u>.) **Il fait lire le livre par l'enfant.** (*He is having* <u>the child</u> *read the book.*)

Laisser faire Construction

The infinitive can also be used after *laisser* (*to let, to allow*) and after verbs of perception such as *entendre* (*to hear*), *voir* (*to see*), *écouter* (*to listen to*), *regarder* (*to watch*), and *sentir* (*to smell, to feel*). As in the *faire faire* construction, the infinitive may have a subject or an object. Notice that the word order is the same: **Je laisse travailler Marie.** (*I'm letting Marie work.*) **Je sens battre mon cœur.** (*I feel my heart beating.*) **J'entends chanter la chanson.** (*I hear the song being sung.*) **Je regarde tourner le film.** (*I am watching the film being made.*) The infinitive may have both a subject and an object. In the *laisser faire* construction, the subject precedes the infinitive and the object follows: **Je laisse Marie finir le travail.** (*I am letting Marie finish the work.*) **J'écoute ma mère chanter un air.** (*I listen to my mother sing a tune.*)

In older texts, the last construction may be the same as *faire faire*: **J'ai entendu cette chanson chanter à une vieille femme.** (*I heard an old woman sing this song.*)

Other Verbs Followed Directly by an Infinitive

The following verbs may be followed directly by an infinitive: **aimer** (*to love*), **affirmer** (*to affirm*), **aller** (*to go*), **compter** (*to count on*), **croire** (*to believe*), **désirer** (*to desire*), **envoyer** (*to send*), **espérer** (*to hope*), **falloir** (*to be necessary*), **oser** (*to dare*), **paraître** (*to appear*), **penser** (*to think*), **pouvoir** (*to be able, can, may*), **préférer** (*to prefer*), **savoir** (*to know how to*), **sembler** (*to seem*), **souhaiter** (*to wish*), **valoir mieux** (*to be preferable*), **venir** (*to come*), **vouloir** (*to want, to wish*): **Savez-vous jouer de la guitare?** (*Do you know how to play the guitar?*) **Il n'ose pas dire la vérité.** (*He doesn't dare tell the truth.*) **Il vaut mieux partir.** (*We had better leave.*)

Verbs Followed by Prepositions before an Infinitive

à **aider** (*to help*), **apprendre** (*to learn*), **arriver** (*to succeed in*), **s'attendre** (*to look forward*), **avoir** (*to have to*), **chercher** (*to look for a way to*), **commencer** (*to begin*), **consentir** (*to agree, to consent to*), **continuer** (*to continue*), **enseigner** (*to teach*), **s'habituer** (*to get accustomed*), **hésiter** (*to hesitate*), **inviter** (*to invite*), **se mettre** (*to begin*),

parvenir (*to succeed in*), **penser** (*to think about*), **persister** (*to persist in*), **se plaire** (*to amuse oneself*), **pousser** (*to push into*), **se préparer** (*to get ready*), **renoncer** (*to renounce*), **se résigner** (*to resign oneself*), **réussir** (*to succeed in*), **servir** (*to be used for*), **songer** (*to dream about*), **tarder** (*to delay*), **tendre** (*to tend*), **tenir** (*to insist on*): **Il apprend à chanter.** (*He is learning to sing.*) **Il a commencé à neiger.** (*It began to snow.*) **Tu réussis à le faire.** (*You are succeeding in doing it.*) **Il m'a invité à dîner.** (*He invited me to have dinner.*)

de accepter (*to accept*), **accuser** (*to accuse*), **achever** (*to finish*), **s'agir** (*to be a question of*), **s'arrêter** (*to stop*), **cesser** (*to cease*), **charger** (*to put in charge of*), **choisir** (*to choose*), **commander** (*to command*), **convenir** (*to agree*), **craindre** (*to fear*), **défendre** (*to forbid*), **se dépêcher** (*to hurry*), **dire** (*to say, to tell*), **empêcher** (*to prevent*), **essayer** (*to attempt*), **éviter** (*to avoid*), **finir** (*to finish*), **se garder** (*to keep from*), **se hâter** (*to hasten*), **interdire** (*to prohibit*), **jurer** (*to swear*), **manquer** (*to fail*), **menacer** (*to threaten*), **mériter** (*to deserve*), **négliger** (*to neglect*), **offrir** (*to offer*), **ordonner** (*to order*), **oublier** (*to forget*), **parler** (*to speak about*), **se passer** (*to do without*), **permettre** (*to permit*), **persuader** (*to persuade*), **prier** (*to ask, to beg*), **promettre** (*to promise*), **proposer** (*to propose*), **refuser** (*to refuse*), **regretter** (*to regret*), **se réjouir** (*to be glad*), **résoudre** (*to resolve*), **rêver** (*to dream about*), **risquer** (*to risk*), **soupçonner** *to suspect of*), **se souvenir** (*to remember*), **tâcher** (*to try*), **tenter** (*to attempt*), **venir** (*to have just*): **Elle lui a dit de le faire.** (*She told him to do it.*) **Nous avons essayé de faire du ski.** (*We tried to ski.*) **Je vous prie de m'aider.** (*I beg you to help me.*) **Il m'interdit de fumer.** (*He forbids me to smoke.*)

à or **de** Some verbs take *à* or *de*, often with different shades of meaning: **Il demande à venir.** (*He asks to come. Demander* has no complement; he wants to come.) **Il me demande de venir.** (*He asks me to come.*) *Demander* has a complement; he wants me to come.) **J'ai décidé de venir.** (*I decided to come. Décider* has no complement; I made the decision.) **Je l'ai décidé à venir.** (*I persuaded him to come. Décider* has a complement; he made the decision.) **Je suis forcé de venir.** (*I am forced to come. Forcer* is used in the passive voice.) **Il me force à venir.** (*He forces me to come. Forcer* is used in the active voice and has a complement.) **Je suis obligé de venir.** (*I am obligated to come. Obliger is used in the passive voice.*) **Il m'oblige à venir.** (*He forces me to come. Obliger is used in the active voice and has a complement.*)

The Passive Voice

The "Pure Passive" with *être*

The passive voice is constructed with a form of the verb *être* and the past participle of a transitive verb—that is, a verb that can take a direct object. The past participle agrees in number and gender with the subject. The tense of the passive is that of the form of *être* used. Because only transitive verbs occur in the passive voice, there can be no confusion with verbs whose compound tenses are conjugated with *être*, as these verbs are all intransitive: **Les lettres ont été distribuées par le facteur.** (*The letters were delivered by the letter carrier.*) **Cette lettre a été envoyée par Marie.** (*This letter was sent by Marie.*) **Les maisons seront construites par un architecte.** (*The houses will be built by a architect.*)

As the above examples illustrate, the agent is usually introduced by the preposition *par* (*by*). A few verbs, however, require *de*, including: **Le professeur est aimé de tous ses étudiants.** (*The professor is loved by all his students.*) **La montagne est couverte de neige.** (*The mountain is covered with snow.*) **Le jardin est entouré d'un mur.** (*The garden is surrounded by a wall.*)

✳ Note!

Since only verbs that take direct objects can be constructed in the "pure passive," verbs that take indirect or prepositional complements are made "passive" by use of the impersonal pronoun *on*: **On a répondu à la lettre.** (*The letter was answered.*) **On donnera l'argent à Jean.** (*Jean will be given the money.*)

Alternatives to the Passive Voice

French speakers tend to avoid the "pure passive" and adopt alternative constructions.

active voice Sentences that an English speaker might construct as passive often are expressed in the active voice in French: **Ce livre a été écrit par un grand auteur.** (*This book was written by a great author.*) > **Un grand auteur a écrit ce livre.** (*A great author wrote this book.*)

on Especially when an agent is not expressed, the "passive" may be expressed by use of the impersonal pronoun *on*: **La lettre est envoyée.** (*The letter is being sent.*) > **On envoie la lettre.** (*The letter is being sent.*) **J'étais admiré.** (*I was admired.*) > **On m'admirait.** (*I was admired.*)

se Verbs in the third person are commonly made "passive" by use of a reflexive construction: **Le gouvernement se compose de trois parties.** (*The government is composed of three branches.*) **Les cravates se vendent ici/On vend les cravates ici.** (*Ties are sold here.*) **Le français se parle partout/On parle français partout.** (*French is spoken everywhere.*) **Cela ne se fait pas/On ne fait pas cela.** (*That is not done.*)

Chapter 6
INTERROGATIVE WORDS AND CONSTRUCTIONS

IN THIS CHAPTER:

✔ *Forming Questions*
✔ *Interrogative Forms by Inversion*
✔ *Interrogative Adverbs and Adverbial Expressions*
✔ Qui? *and* Que?
✔ Quel?
✔ Lequel?

Forming Questions

Questions are formed in French in the following ways:

1. by changing the period of a statement to a question mark and, in speech, using a rising intonation: **Elle parle français. > Elle parle français?** (*She speaks French?*) **Il se réveille. > Il se réveille?** (*He's waking up?*)

2. by adding *n'est-ce pas?* to a statement to imply that the speaker expects an answer in the affirmative: **Tu vas au musée** > **Tu vas au musée, n'est-ce pas?** (*You're going to the museum, aren't you?*) **Il est arrivé.** > **Il est arrivé, n'est-ce pas?** (*He has arrived, hasn't he?*)

3. by adding *est-ce que* (*est-ce qu'* before vowels and mute *h*) at the beginning of a statement and changing the period to a question mark: **Pierre nous parlera.** > **Est-ce que Pierre nous parlera?** (*Will Pierre speak to us?*) **Elle s'est bien habillée.** > **Est-ce qu'elle s'est bien habillée?** (*Did she dress well?*)

4. By inverting the subject and the verb.

Interrogative Forms by Inversion

Simple Inversion of Subject Pronouns

Questions may be formed by inverting a subject pronoun and the verb of a declarative sentence. In compound tenses, only the auxiliary is inverted. The subject pronoun is joined to the verb by a hyphen: **Tu vas à Londres?** > **Vas-tu à Londres?** (*Are you going to London?*) **Nous nous levons.** > **Nous levons-nous?** (*Are we getting up?*) **Il écrit une lettre.** > **Écrit-il une lettre?** (*Is he writing a letter?*) **Elles sont allées à Toronto.** > **Sont-elles allées à Toronto?** (*Did they go to Toronto?*) **Il s'est couché.** > **S'est-il couché?** (*Did he go to bed?*)

When inverting a 3rd singular subject pronoun and verb, a *t* is inserted between the verb and the pronoun if the verb ends in a vowel; the *t* is connected to the pronoun and to the verb with hyphens. This occurs in First Conjugation verbs plus *aller* and *avoir* in the present indicative; in all future and future perfects; in the *passé composé* of verbs conjugated with *avoir*; and in the *passé simple* of First Conjugation Verbs: **Il parle français.** > **Parle-t-il français?** (*Does he speak French?*) **Elle a de l'argent.** > **A-t-elle de l'argent?** (*Does she have any money?*) **On finira à l'heure.** > **Finira-t-on à l'heure?** (*Will they finish on time?*) **Elle a visité Vancouver.** > **A-t-elle visité Vancouver?** (*Has she visited Vancouver?*)

Inversion is usually not used in the 1st singular except in formal writing. French speakers use *est-ce que* instead: **Je suis content.** > **Est-ce que je suis content?** (*Am I happy?*) When a First Conjugation verb is inverted in the 1st singular in writing, an acute accent is added to the final –*e*: **J'ose espérer qu'il vit.** > **Osé-je espérer qu'il vit?** (*Dare I hope that he is alive?*) In the 1st singular, inversion may occur with certain often-used verbs in fixed expressions (note that *pouvoir* has the special form *puis*): **Puis-je vous servir du café?** (*May I serve you some coffee?*) **Que sais-je?** (*What do I know?*)

Complex Inversion

When inverting with a noun subject, the noun is stated first, as in a declarative sentence, then a pronoun is introduced in inverted position: **Marie parle français.** > **Marie parle-t-elle français?** (*Does Marie speak French?*) **Les Françaises sont chic.** > **Les Françaises sont-elles chic?** (*Are French women stylish?*) **Vos enfants seront sages.** > **Vos enfants seront-ils sages?** (*Will your children be good?*) **Jean a eu peur.** > **Jean a-t-il eu peur?** (*Did Jean become frightened?*)

Interrogative Adverbs and Adverbial Expressions

The following are common interrogative adverbs and adverbial expressions used to introduce questions: **A quelle heure?** (*At what time?*), **Combien?** (*How much? How many?*), **Comment?** (*How?*), **Pourquoi?** (*Why*), **Où?** (*Where?*), **Quand?** (*When?*)

In formulating questions with these interrogatives, either *est-ce que* or inversion may be used. The use of *est-ce que* is more conversational, while inversion is more elegant: **A quelle heure vient-il?/A quelle heure est-ce qu'il vient?** (*What time is he coming?*) **Quand est-il né?/Quand est-ce qu'il est né?** (*When was he born?*) **Pourquoi ne vient-il pas?/Pourquoi est-ce qu'il ne vient pas?** (*Why isn't he coming?*) **Comment ont-ils gagné?/Comment est-ce qu'ils ont gagné?** (*How did they win?*)

In certain very common expressions, only inversion is used: **Comment allez-vous?** (*How are you?*) **Comment va-t-il?** (*How is he?*)

Combien can modify a verb or, with *de*, be used as an expression of quantity: **Combien coûte-t-il?**/**Combien est-ce qu'il coûte?** *(How much does it cost?)* **Combien d'autos vendez-vous?**/**Combien d'autos est-ce que vous vendez?** *(How many cars do you sell?)*

When a noun subject is expressed with *à quelle heure, pourquoi,* and *combien de,* either *est-ce que* or complex inversion may be used: **Pourquoi Jean ne travaille-t-il pas?**/**Pourquoi est-ce que Jean ne travaille pas?** *(Why doesn't Jean work?)* **A quelle heure les invités viendront-ils?**/**A quelle heure est-ce que les invités viendront?** *(At what time will the guests come?)* **Combien de livres Marie possède-t-elle?**/**Combien de livres est-ce que Marie possède?** *(How many books does Marie possess?)*

When a noun subject is expressed, *combien* (without *de*), *comment, où,* and *quand* may introduce a special type of simple inversion of noun and verb: **Combien coûte le biftek?**/**Combien le biftek coûte-t-il?**/**Combien est-ce que le biftek coûte?** *(How much does the steak cost?)* **Où va Marie?**/**Où Marie va-t-elle?**/**Où est-ce que Marie va?** *(Where is Marie going?)* **Quand viendront les invités?**/**Quand les invités viendront-ils?**/**Quand est-ce que les invités viendront?** *(When will the guests come?)* **Comment est l'église?**/**Comment l'église est-elle?** *(What does the church look like?)*

Qui? and Que?

As Subjects and Direct Complements of Verbs

Interrogative pronouns have long and short forms. As <u>subject</u> of the verb, however, the impersonal *(What?)* does not have a short form: **Qui? Qu'est-ce qui?** *(Who?)*: **Qui vient?**/**Qui est-ce qui vient?** *(Who is coming?)***Qu'est-ce qui?** *(What?)*: **Qu'est-ce qui arrive?** *(What is happening?)*

As the <u>object</u> of the verb, the short form requires inversion; notice that the long form already contains *est-ce que*: **Qui? Qui est-ce que?** *(Whom?)*: **Qui voit-elle?**/ **Qui est-ce qu'elle voit?** *(Whom does she see?)* **Que? Qu'est-ce que?** *(What?)*: **Que fait-il?**/ **Qu'est-ce qu'il fait?** *(What is he doing?)*

Qui never elides with a vowel: **Qui est il?** *(Who is he?)* **Qui aimez-vous?** *(Whom do you love?)*

Q*ue* and *qu'est-ce que* may be used as predicates: **Qu'est-il sans sa famille?** (*What is he without his family?*)

As Objects of Prepositions

Interrogative pronouns as objects of prepositions are used with inversion or with *est-ce que*. Notice that in French the prepositional phrase comes at the beginning of the sentence and, unlike English usage, the preposition is never separated from its complement: **qui?** (*whom?*): **Avec qui sort-il?/Avec qui est-ce qu'il sort?** (*Who does he go out with?*)**quoi?** (*what?*): **Avec quoi écrit-il?/Avec quoi est-ce qu'il écrit?** (*What does he write with?*)

In complex inversion, the prepositional phrase comes first and is followed by the noun subject; but *est-ce que* precedes the noun: *De qui* **Jean *a-t-il* parlé?/De qui est-ce que Jean a parlé?** (*Whom did Jean talk about?*)**De quoi Marie a-t-elle besoin?/De quoi est-ce que Marie a besoin?** (*What does Marie need?*)

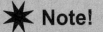

✳ Note!

Quoi? may be used without a preposition in certain fixed expressions: **Quoi de neuf?** (*What's new?*)**Quoi de nouveau?** (*What's new?*)**Quoi? Vous voulez me voir?** (*What? You want to see me?*)

Quel?

The interrogative adjective agrees in number and gender with the noun it modifies. It is translated as *what?* or *which?*

singular: **quel** (masculine), **quelle** (feminine)
plural: **quels** (masculine), **quelles** (feminine)

Qu'est-ce que? and Qu'est-ce que c'est?

These expressions are used to ask for a definition; the longer forms are more familiar: **Qu'est-ce que c'est?** (*What is this? What is that?*) **Qu-est-ce que c'est que cela?** (*What's that?*) **Qu'est-ce que le jeu de boules?** (*What is bocci?*) **Qu'est-ce que c'est que le jeu de boules?** (*What is bocci?*) **Qu'est-ce qu'un dîner sans vin?** (*What is a dinner without wine?*)

Quel serves as the subject of the verb *être*, agreeing with the noun complement; it may also directly modify a noun: **Quel est votre nom?** (*What is your name?*) **Quelle est votre adresse?** (*What is your address?*) **Quels livres lisez-vous?** (*What books are you reading?*) **Quelles cravates achète-t-il?** (*Which ties is he buying?*) **A quelle université enseigne-t-il?** (*At what university does he teach?*) **Avec quels hommes sort-elle?** (*What men does she go out with?*)

Quel used with *être* in reference to a person asks for an identification such as a person's occupation: **Quels sont ces hommes? Ce sont des médecins.** (*What are these men? They're physicians.*)

Quel is used in elliptical sentences: **Regarde ce garçon. Quel garçon?** (*Look at that boy. What boy?*) **J'ai vu des amis. Quels amis?** (*I saw some friends. Which friends?*)

Quel is also used in exclamations: **Quel garçon!** (*What a boy!*) **Quelle belle femme!** (*What a beautiful woman!*) **Quels bons joueurs!** (*What good players!*)

Lequel?

The interrogative *lequel?* asks *which one?* or *which ones?* out of a specified group of people or things. It agrees in number and gender with the noun used to name the members of the group. Note that it is constructed with the definite article combined with the interrogative *quel?*

singular: **lequel** (masculine), **laquelle** (feminine)
plural: **lesquels** (masculine), **lesquelles** (feminine)

Lequel de ces livres voulez-vous? (*Which one of these books do you want?*) **Lesquels** de ces livres voulez-vous? (*Which ones of these books do you want?*) **Laquelle** de ces peintures préférez-vous? (*Which one of these paintings do you prefer?*) **Lesquelles** de ces peintures voulez-vous? (*Which ones of these paintings do you want?*) The forms of *lequel* contract with the prepositions *à* and *de*:

masculine: **auquel, auxquels; duquel, desquels**
feminine: **à laquelle, auxquelles; de laquelle, desquelles**

Auquel de ces garçons parliez-vous? (*Which one of these boys were you talking to?*) **Desquelles** de ces femmes a-t-il parlé? (*Which ones of these women did he talk about?*)

The forms of *lequel* may stand by themselves: **J'ai de bons livres. Lesquels?** (*I have some good books. Which ones?*) **Je voudrais de ces pommes. Lesquelles?** (*I would like some of these apples. Which ones?*)

Chapter 7
NEGATIVE WORDS AND CONSTRUCTIONS

IN THIS CHAPTER:

✔ *Negation of Simple Tenses*
✔ *Negation of Compound Tenses*
✔ *The Negative Interrogative*
✔ Si *in Answer to a Negative Question*
✔ *Negation of the Infinitive*
✔ *Other Negative Words and Phrases*
✔ *The Partitive and Indefinite Article after a Negative Expression*

Negation of Simple Tenses

Verbs in simple tenses are made negative by placing *ne* (*n'* before a vowel or mute *h*) before the verb and *pas* after it: **Il parle français.** > **Il ne parle pas français. Nous lisons beaucoup.** > **Nous ne lisons pas beaucoup. Elle écrira le poème.** > **Elle n'écrira pas le poème. A ta place, je viendrais.** > **A ta place, je ne viendrais pas.**

In forming the negative of reflexive verbs, *ne* is placed before the reflexive pronoun: **Je me réveille.** > **Je ne me réveille pas. Il s'habillera bien.** > **Il ne s'habillera pas bien. Nous nous couchions tard.** > **Nous ne nous couchions pas tard.**

In sentences with a verb followed by a complementary infinitive, it is normally the main verb that is negated: **Il veut venir.** > **Il ne veut pas venir. J'aime faire du ski.** > **Je n'aime pas faire du ski. Elle va se lever.** > **Elle ne va pas se lever.**

Negation of Compound Tenses

Verbs in compound tenses are made negative by adding *ne* (*n'*) before and *pas* after the auxiliary *avoir* or *être*: **J'ai fini.** > **Je n'ai pas fini. Elle est venue.** > **Elle n'est pas venue. Nous serons arrivés.** > **Nous ne serons pas arrivés. Elles étaient venues.** > **Elles n'étaient pas venues. Nous aurions fait cela.** > **Nous n'aurions pas fait cela.**

In forming the negative of reflexive verbs, *ne* is placed before the reflexive pronoun: **Elle s'est levée.** > **Elle ne s'est pas levée. Je me serai bien habillée.** > **Je ne me serai pas bien habillée.**

The Negative Interrogative

In the simple tenses, *ne* (*n'*) is placed before the verb and *pas* after the verb or, when inversion is used, after a pronoun subject attached to the verb with hyphens: **Marie travaille?** > **Marie ne travaille pas? Est-ce qu'elle se réveille?** > **Est ce qu'elle ne se réveille pas? Il se rase,** n'est-ce pas? > Il <u>ne</u> se rase <u>pas</u>, n'est-ce pas? Travaille-t-il? > <u>Ne</u> travaille-t-il <u>pas</u> Jean va-t-il à Paris? > Jean <u>ne</u> va-t-il <u>pas</u> à Paris?

In compound tenses, *ne* (*n'*) is placed before the auxiliary and *pas* after the auxiliary or, when inversion is used, after a pronoun subject attached to the auxiliary with hyphens: **Avez-vous fini?** > **N'avez-vous <u>pas</u> fini? Es-tu partie?** > **<u>N'</u>es-tu pas partie? Est-ce qu'il a parlé?** > **Est-ce qu'il <u>n'</u>a <u>pas</u> parlé? Il s'est amusé, n'est-ce pas?** > **Il <u>ne</u> s'est <u>pas</u> amusé, n'est-ce pas?**

For reflexive verbs, *ne* (*n'*) precedes the reflexive pronoun: **Vous couchez-vous?** > **<u>Ne</u> vous couchez-vous <u>pas</u>? Se sont-elles levées?** > **<u>Ne</u> se sont-elles pas <u>levées</u>?Jean s'est-il réveillé?** > **Jean <u>ne</u> s'est-il <u>pas</u> réveillé?**

Si in Answer to a Negative Question

When answering a negative question in the affirmative in order to contradict its negative implication, *si* is used instead of *oui*: **Ne parles-tu pas français? Si, je parle français.** (*Don't you speak French? Yes, I do speak French.*)**Tu ne viendras pas, n'est-ce pas? Si, je viendrai.** (*You won't come, will you? Yes, I will come.*)

In answering negative questions, *oui* implies agreement: **Tu ne viendras pas, n'est-ce pas? Oui, je ne viendrai pas.** (*You won't come, will you? No, I won't come.*)

✸ Important Point!

Omission of *Pas*

In writing especially, *pas* may be omitted in negating *savoir* (*to know*), *pouvoir* (*to be able, may, can*), *oser* (*to dare*), *cesser* (*to cease*):
Il <u>ne</u> sait que faire. (*He doesn't know what to do.*) **Je <u>ne</u> peux vous comprendre.** (*I cannot understand you.*) **Ils <u>n'</u>osent faire cela.** (*They don't dare do that.*) **Il <u>ne</u> cesse de neiger.**(*It doesn't stop snowing.*)

Negation of the Infinitive

To make an infinitive negative, *ne pas* is placed before it: **Il me dit de ne pas pleurer.** (*He tells me not to cry.*) When there is a pronoun complement, *ne pas* precedes the pronoun: **Il me dit de ne pas me coucher.** (*He tells me not to go to bed.*) **Je vous dis de ne pas y aller.** (*I'm telling you not to go there.*) With the past infinitive, *pas* may follow the auxiliary: **Elle affirme ne pas avoir fait ses devoirs/Elle affirme n'avoir pas fait ses devoirs.** (*She affirms that she did not do her homework.*) **Elle croit ne pas s'être couchée avant minuit/Elle croit ne s'être pas couchée avant minuit.** (*She believes that she didn't go to bed before midnight.*)

Other Negative Words and Phrases

Many negative expressions function like *ne . . . pas.*
1. *ne . . . pas du tout* (*not at all*): **Il n'est pas du tout bête.** (*He's not at all stupid.*)
2. *ne . . . point* (*not* [emphatic, but also dated]): **Il ne dit point cela.** (*He does not say that.*)
3. *ne . . . plus (de)* (*no longer, no more*): **Il ne travaille plus.** (*He doesn't work any more.*) **Je n'ai plus d'argent.** (*I have no more money.*)
4. *ne . . . jamais* (*never*): **Il n'oubliera jamais ce film.** (*He'll never forget this film.*) **Je n'ai jamais été en France.** (*I have never been to France.*) For emphasis: **Jamais je n'y retournerai.** (*I'll never go back there.*) *Jamais* may stand alone: **Tu abandonnes? Jamais!** (*Do you give up? Never!*) *Jamais* without *ne* means "ever": **As-tu jamais été en France?** (*Have you ever been to France?*) *Jamais* is the negative expression that replaces *toujours*: **Elle y va toujours.** (*She always goes there.*) **Elle n'y va jamais.** (*She never goes there.*)
5. *ne . . . guère* (*hardly*): **Il n'a guère le temps.** (*He hardly has the time.*)
6. *ne . . . aucun(e)* (*not any*): **Il n'a aucun livre.** (*He has not a single book.*) **Je n'ai aucune idée.** (*I have no idea.*) **Il n'a planté aucun arbre.** (*He did not plant any trees.*) Also as a pronoun: **Aucun de ses amis ne sait.** (*Not one of his friends knows.*) **Je ne vois aucune de ses autos.** (*I don't see any of his cars.*) *Aucun* in the negative expression

that replaces *quelque(s)*: **J'ai quelques problèmes.** (*I have some problems.*) **Je n'ai aucun problème.** (*I don't have a single problem.*)
7. *ne . . . plus aucun(e)* (*no longer any*): **Il n'a plus aucun ami.** (*He no longer has any friends.*)
8. *ne . . . que* (*only*): **Il n'a que deux chambres.** (*He has only two bedrooms.*)
9. *ne . . . plus que* (*only . . . any more*): **Je n'ai plus qu'un sou.** (*I have only one penny left.*) **Il n'a plus que des dettes.** (*All he has any more is debts.*)
10. *ne . . . rien* (*nothing*): **Il ne voit rien.** (*He sees nothing.*) **Je n'ai rien compris.** (*I didn't understand anything.*) *Rien* may stand by itself: **Qu'as-tu fait? Rien.** (*What did you do? Nothing.*) *Rien* may serve as the subject of a verb: **Rien ne m'est arrivé.** (*Nothing happened to me.*) *Rien* may be modified by an invariable adjective introduced by *de*: **Je n'ai fait rien d'illégal.** (*I didn't do anything illegal.*) **Rien d'horrible ne s'est passé.** (*Nothing horrible happened.*)
Rien is the negative expression that replaces *quelque chose*: **Je vois quelque chose.** (*I see something.*) **Je ne vois rien.** (*I see nothing.*)
11. *ne . . . personne* (*no one*): **Il n'aime personne.** (*He loves no one.*) **Elle n'a vu personne.** (*She did not see anyone.*) *Personne* may stand by itself: **Qui vois-tu? Personne.** (*Whom do you see? No one.*) *Personne* may serve as the subject of a verb: **Personne ne lui a téléphoné.** (*No one phoned him.*) *Personne* may be modified by an invariable adjective introduced by *de*: **Personne d'important ne vient.** (*No one important is coming.*) **Je ne connais personne d'âgé.** (*I know no one who is old.*) *Personne* is the negative expression that replaces *quelqu'un*: **Je vois quelqu'un.** (*I see someone.*) **Je ne vois personne.** (*I don't see anyone.*)
12. *ne . . . nul(le)* (*no, not any*): **Il n'a nulle autorité ici.** (*He has no authority here.*) **Nul livre ne l'intéresse.** (*No book interests him.*)
Nul may stand as a pronoun: **Nul ne sait la vérité.** (*No one knows the truth.*)
13. *ne . . . nulle part* (*nowhere*): **Je ne vais nulle part.** (*I'm not going anywhere.*)
14. *ne . . . ni . . . ni* (*neither . . . nor*): **Il n'a ni père ni mère.** (*He has neither father nor mother.*) **Il n'écrit ni à son père ni à sa mère.** (*He writes neither his father nor his mother.*) **Je ne sais ni lire ni écrire.** (*I can neither read nor write.*) **Il ne veut ni chanter ni jouer ni étudier ni manger.** (*He doesn't want to sing or to play or to study or to eat.*)

15. Ni l'un(e) ni l'autre . . . ne (neither one nor the other): <u>Ni l'une ni l'autre</u> de mes sœurs <u>ne</u> m'écrit. *(Neither one of my sisters writes to me.)* Voilà pourquoi je <u>n'aime ni l'une ni l'autre.</u> *(That's why I don't like either one of them.)*

16. *non plus (either, neither):* *Non plus* is the negative expression that replaces *aussi:* Il le sait. Je le sais aussi. *(He knows it. I know it too.)* Il ne le sait pas. Je ne le sais pas <u>non plus.</u> *(He does not know it. I don't know it either.)* Il pense beaucoup. Moi aussi. *(He thinks a lot. I do too.)* Il ne pense pas beaucoup. <u>(Ni)</u> <u>moi non plus.</u> *(He doesn't think a lot. I don't either.)*

The Partitive and Indefinite Article after a Negative Expression

Remember that after verbs negated with *pas, jamais,* or *plus,* both the partitive and the indefinite article become *de* (*d'* before vowels or mute *h*): J'ai de l'argent. *(I have money.)* Je n'ai pas d'argent. *(I have no money.)* J'ai une maison. *(I have a house.)* Je n'ai pas de maison. *(I don't have a house.)* J'ai des livres. *(I have some books.)* Je n'ai plus de livres. *(I don't have any books any more.)* Je prends des tomates. *(I'm eating tomatoes.)* Je ne prends jamais de tomates. *(I never eat tomatoes.)* However, after *ne . . . que,* the partitive and the indefinite article are used: J'ai du vin. *(I have wine.)* Je n'ai que du vin. *(I have only wine.)* Je lis des journaux. *(I read newspapers.)* Je ne lis que des journaux. *(I read only newspapers.)*

Chapter 8
PRONOUNS

IN THIS CHAPTER:

✔ *Subject Pronouns*
✔ *Object Pronouns*
✔ *Disjunctive Pronouns*
✔ *Possessive Pronouns*
✔ *Indefinite Demonstrative Pronouns*
✔ *Relative Pronouns*
✔ *Indefinite Pronouns*

Subject Pronouns

The subject personal pronouns are:

	singular	plural
1st person	**je** (**j'** before a vowel or mute *h*)	**nous**
2nd person	**tu**	**vous**
3rd person	**il** (masculine)	**ils**
	elle (feminine)	**elles**
	on (impersonal)	

For detailed discussion, see the introduction to Chap. 5.

Object Pronouns

Direct Object Personal Pronouns

Me, Te, Nous, and *Vous*

The 1st person direct object pronouns are *me* (*m'* before a vowel or mute *h*) (singular) and *nous* (plural); the 2nd person forms are *te* (*t'* before a vowel or mute *h*) (singular) and *vous* (plural). In simple tenses these pronoun objects are placed immediately before the verb: **Il me voit.** (*He sees me.*) **Me voit-il?** (*Does he see me?*) **Elle te regarde.** (*She looks at you.*) **Ne te regarde-t-elle pas?** (*Isn't she looking at you?*) **Elle ne te regarde pas.** (*She is not looking at you.*) **Est-ce qu'elle nous comprend?** (*Does she understand us?*) **Elle ne nous comprend pas.** (*She doesn't understand us.*) **Je vous regarde.** (*I'm looking at you.*) **Je ne vous regarde pas.** (*I'm not looking at you.*)

Le, La, and *Les*

The 3rd person direct object pronouns are *le* (masculine singular), *la* (feminine singular), and *les* (plural, both genders); *le* and *la* become *l'* before vowels and mute *h*. These pronoun objects are placed immediately before the verb: **Jean lit-il le livre?** (*Is Jean reading the book?*) **Jean le lit-il?** (*Is Jean reading it?*) **Pierre ne regarde pas la maison.** (*Pierre is not looking at the house.*) **Pierre ne la regarde pas.** (*Pierre is not looking at it.*) **Voit-il les nuages?** (*Does he see the clouds.*) **Les voit-il?** (*Does he see them?*) **Marie adore-t-elle Marc?** (*Does Marie adore Marc?*) **Marie l'adore-t-elle?** (*Does Marie adore him?*) **Marc aime Marie.** (*Marc loves Marie.*) **Marc l'aime.** (*Marc loves her.*)

Indirect Object Personal Pronouns

Me, Te, Nous, and *Vous*

In the 1st and 2nd persons, the forms of the indirect object are identical to the forms of the direct object. Like the direct object forms, the

You Need to Know ✔

Special Use of the Pronoun *Le*

Le (*l'*) can be used to replace a complete idea, such as a noun clause or an adjective: **Croyez-vous qu'il arrive ce soir?** (*Do you believe he'll arrive tonight?*) **Le croyez-vous?** (*Do you believe it?*) **Oui, je le crois.** (*Yes, I believe so.*) *Le* is used regardless of the gender and number of the adjective it replaces: **Je suis content, ils le sont aussi.** (*I am happy; they are happy too.*) **Je suis content, elle le sera aussi.** (*I am happy; she will be too.*)

indirect object pronoun immediately precedes the verb: **Me parle-t-il?** (*Does he speak to me?*) **Elle ne m'écrit jamais.** (*She never writes to me.*) **Elle te pose une question.** (*She's asking you a question.*) **Il nous donne les livres.** (*He gave the books to us.*) **Je ne vous donne pas d'argent.** (*I am not giving you any money.*)

Lui and *Leur*

In the 3rd person, the forms of the indirect object are *lui* (singular, both genders) and *leur* (plural). These pronouns immediately precede the verb: **Est-ce que je parle à Pierre?** (*Am I speaking to Pierre?*) **Est-ce que je lui parle?** (*Am I speaking to him?*) **Je ne donne pas le livre à Marie.** (*I am not giving to book to Marie.*) **Je ne lui donne pas le livre.** (*I am not giving her the book.*) **Nous écrivons à Hélène.** (*We are writing to Hélène.*) **Nous lui écrivons.** (*We're writing to her.*) **Parle-t-elle aux garçons?** (*Is she speaking to the boys?*) **Leur parle-t-elle?** (*Is she speaking to them?*) **Tu ne réponds pas aux filles?** (*You don't answer the girls?*) **Tu ne leur réponds pas?** (*You don't answer them?*)

The Pronoun Y

The pronoun *y* can replace a prepositional phrase beginning with any preposition other than *de* when the object of the preposition is a place or a thing. When the object is a place, *y* means "there." *Y* immediately precedes the verb: **Je vais à la gare.** (*I'm going to the train station.*) **J'y vais.** (*I'm going there.*) **N'est-elle pas dans le salon?** (*Isn't she in the living room?*) **N'y est-elle pas?** (*Isn't she there?*) **Il met son argent sur la table.** (*He puts his money on the table.*) **Il y met son argent.** (*He puts his money there.*) **Ne répondons-nous pas à la lettre?** (*Aren't we answering the letter?*) **N'y répondons-nous pas?** (*Aren't we answering it?*) **Je fais attention aux feux rouges.** (*I pay attention to traffic lights.*) **J'y fais attention.** (*I pay attention to them.*)

The Pronoun *En*

The pronoun *en* replaces a prepositional phrase introduced by *de*. *En* immediately precedes the verb. It is used:

1. in adverb phrases: **Nous venons de New York.** (*We come from New York.*) **Nous en venons.** (*We come from there.*) **Ils ne partent pas de Paris.** (*They are not leaving from Paris.*) **Ils n'en partent pas.** (*They are not leaving from there.*)

2. in a partitive sense: **J'ai du pain.** (*I have bread.*) **J'en ai.** (*I have some.*) **Tu ne veux pas de crème?** (*You don't want any cream?*) **Tu n'en veux pas?** (*You don't want any?*)

3. as an indefinite: **Je n'ai pas de livre.** (*I don't have a book.*) **Je n'en ai pas.** (*I don't have one.*) **Vous avez des pommes?** (*You have apples?*) **Vous en avez?** (*You have some?*) **Ils n'ont pas d'enfants.** (*They have no children.*) **Ils n'en ont pas.** (*They don't have any.*)

4. with expressions of quantity: **Il a beaucoup de voitures.** (*He has many cars.*) **Il en a beaucoup.** (*He has many of them.*) **Je n'ai pas trop de livres.** (*I don't have too many books.*) **Je n'en ai pas trop.** (*I don't have too many.*) **Combien d'enfants as-tu?** (*How many children do you have?*) **Combien en as-tu?** (*How many do you have?*) *En* replaces nouns accompanied by a number: **Elle a dix livres.** (*She has ten books.*) **Elle en a dix.** (*She has ten.*) **Nous avons cinq enfants.** (*We have five children.*) **Nous en avons cinq.** (*We have five.*) *En* replaces nouns modified by *plusieurs*: **Elle a plusieurs amis.** (*She has several friends.*) **Elle**

en a plusieurs. (*She has several.*) *En* replaces nouns modified by *quelques*; notice that *quelques* is transformed: **J'ai quelques disques.** (*I have a few disks.*) **J'en ai quelques-uns.** (*I have a few.* [masculine]) **Il a quelques peintures.** (*He has several paintings.*) **Il en a quelques-unes.** (*He has several.* [feminine])

    5. with expressions dependent on verbs, adjectives, etc.: **Elle parle de ce livre.** (*She is talking about this book.*) **Elle en parle.** (*She is talking about it.*) **Il n'est pas fier du prix.** (*He is not proud of the prize.*) **Il n'en est pas fier.** (*He is not proud of it.*) **Que penses-tu de ce cas?** (*What do you think of this case?*) **Qu'en penses-tu?** (*What do you think of it?*)

Double Object Pronouns

French verbs can have no more than two pronoun objects, and they must have different functions. Both precede the verb (except in affirmative commands) in the following order:

me			
te	le	lui	
se *precede*	la *precede*	leur *precede*	y *precedes* en
nous	les		
vous			

Me donne-t-il le livre? (*Is he giving me the book?*) **Me le donne-t-il?** (*Is he giving it to me.*) **Il ne me rend pas la disquette.** (*He is not returning the disk to me.*) **Il ne me la rend pas.** (*He is not returning it to me.*) **Il te raconte l'histoire.** (*He is telling you the story.*) **Il te la raconte.** (*He is telling it to you.*) **Elle se rappelle mon numéro.** (*She remembers my number.*) **Elle se le rappelle.** (*She remembers it.*) **Il ne nous montre pas les photos.** (*He does not show us the pictures.*) **Il ne nous les montre pas.** (*He does not show them to us.*) **Je vous écris la lettre.** (*I'm writing you the letter.*) **Je vous l'écris.** (*I'm writing it to you.*) **Je ne le vendrai jamais à Marie.** (*I'll never sell it to Marie.*) **Je ne le lui vendrai jamais.** (*I'll never sell it to her.*) **Elle leur apporte la salade.** (*She brings them the salad.*)

Elle **la leur** apporte. (*She brings it to them.*) Ne **me** donnera-t-il pas **d'argent?** (*Won't he give me any money?*) Ne **m'** en donnera-t-il pas? (*Won't he give me any?*) Elle **lui** vend **des billets**. (*She is selling him tickets.*) Elle **lui en** vend. (*She is selling him some.*) Il **nous** retrouve **au café**. (*He's meeting us at the café.*) Il **nous y** retrouve. (*He's meeting us there.*) Il **y** a quelques **programmes**. (*There are a few programs.*) Il **y en** a quelques-uns. (*There are a few of them.*)

When *me, te, se, nous,* or *vous* is the direct object and another personal pronoun is the indirect object, the indirect object is expressed with *à* followed by a disjunctive pronoun (see below): **Je me suis présenté à elle.** (*I introduced myself to her.*) **Ils me recommande à toi.** (*They recommend me to you.*)

Personal Pronoun Objects in Compound Tenses

Position

Object pronouns immediately precede the auxiliaries *avoir* and, for reflexive verbs, *être*: **Elle leur a apporté la salade.** (*She brought the salad to them.*) **Elle lui a vendu les billets.** (*She sold him the tickets.*) **M'a-t-il donné les photos?** (*Did he give me the pictures?*) **Elle en avait parlé.** (*She had talked about it.*) **Ils se le sont rappelé.** (*They remembered it.*)

Agreement of the Past Participle

The past participle agrees with a direct object preceding the verb, so it agrees in number and gender with the direct object pronouns: **Elle la leur a apportée.** (*She brought it to them.*) **Elle les lui a vendus.** (*She sold them to him.*) **Me les a-t-il données?** (*Did he give them to me?*) **Il nous a vus.** (*He saw us.*) **Nous la leur avons écrite.** (*We wrote it to them.*)

Agreement does not occur with *en*, however: **Elle lui a vendu des billets.** (*She sold him some tickets.*) **Elle lui en a vendu.** (*She sold him some.*)

Pronoun Objects with Infinitive Constructions

Causative *faire* (*faire faire*) and *laisser faire* Constructions

In the causative *faire* (*faire faire*) construction (*See* Chap. 5), all complements precede the conjugated form of *faire*: **Je fais construire ma maison**. (*I'm having my house built*.) **Je la fais construire**. (*I'm having it built*.) **Je la fais construire à mon frère**. (*I'm having my brother build it*.) **Je la lui fais construire**. (*I'm having him build it*.) **Il fait cuire du pain**. (*He is baking bread*.) **Il en fait cuire**. (*He is baking some*.) **Il en fait cuire à ses enfants**. (*He's making his children bake some*.)**Il leur en fait cuire**. (*He's making them bake some*.)

In the compound tenses, the past participle of *faire* does not agree with any of the complements. **J'ai fait construire ma maison**. > **Je l'ai fait construire**. **Je l'ai fait construire à mon frère**. > **Je la lui ai fait construire**. **J'ai fait lire les filles**. > **Je les ai fait lire**.

In the *laisser faire* construction (*See* Chap. 5), a single complement precedes the conjugated verb regardless of its function. **Je laisse travailler les étudiants**. (*I'm letting the students work*.) **Je les laisse travailler**. (*I'm letting them work*.) **J'entends chanter la chanson**. (*I hear the song being sung*.) **Je l'entends chanter**. (*I'm hearing it sung*.) **Je sens battre mon cœur**. (*I feel my heart beating*.) **Je le sens battre**. (*I feel it beating*.) **Je regarde jouer ma fille**. (*I'm watching my daughter play*.) **Je la regarde jouer**. (*I'm watching her play*.)

In the *laisser faire* construction, when there are two complements, the subject of the infinitive precedes the conjugated verb and the complement of the infinitive precedes the infinitive: **Je regarde ma fille jouer ses jeux**. (*I'm watching my daughter play her games*.) **Je la regarde jouer ses jeux**. (*I'm watching her play her games*.) **Je regarde ma fille les jouer**. (*I'm watching my daughter play them*.) **Je vois ma mère faire la tarte**. (*I see my mother making a pie*.) **Je la vois faire la tarte**. (*I see her making the pie*.) **Je vois ma mère la faire**. (*I see my mother making it*.)

In the compound tenses, the past participle agrees with a pronoun object only if it is the subject of the infinitive: **J'ai laissé travailler les enfants**. (*I let the children work*.) **Je les ai laissés travailler**. (*I let them work*.) **J'ai regardé jouer ma fille**. (*I watched my daughter playing*.) **Je l'ai regardée jouer**. (*I watched her playing*.)But: **J'ai entendu chanter la chanson**.(*I heard the song being sung*.) **Je l'ai entendu chanter**. (*I heard it being sung*.)

✴ Note!

Other Infinitive Constructions

When pronoun are the objects of an infinitive in other constructions, they immediately precede the infinitive: **Je vais acheter la disquette.** (*I'm going to buy the diskette.*) **Je vais l'acheter.** (*I'm going to buy it.*) **Il veut parler de cela à Jean.** (*He wants to talk to Jean about that.*) **Il veut lui en parler.** (*He wants to talk to him about it.*) **Elle me dit d'acheter les livres.** (*She tells me to buy the books.*) **Elle me dit de les acheter.** (*She tells me to buy them.*)

Pronoun Complements with Affirmative Imperatives

In negative commands, pronoun objects precede the verb, which is the normal word order: **Ne les écoutez pas.** (*Don't listen to them.*) **Ne m' en parle jamais.** (*Don't ever talk to me about it.*)

In affirmative commands, however, pronoun objects follow the verb and are attached to it by hyphens. No more than two objects, each with a different function, may be used at one time. The appropriate order is: **direct object** *precedes* **indirect object** *precedes y precedes en* **Donnons du pain aux enfants.** (*Let's give the children some bread.*) **Donnons-leur-en.** (*Let's give them some.*) **Vends la maison à Jean.** (*Sell the house to Jean.*) **Vends-la-lui.** (*Sell it to him.*)

If the last word in the sequence would be *me* or *te*, the forms *moi* and *toi* are used: **Regardez-moi.** (*Look at me.*) **Lève-toi.** (*Get up.*) **Donnez-les-moi.** (*Give them to me.*)

However, if *y* or *en* follows, *me* and *te* elide: **Donne-m'en.** (*Give me some.*) **Achète-t'en.** (*Buy some for yourself.*)

Before *y* and *en* an *s* is added to the 2nd singular imperative form of -er verbs: **Achètes-en.** (*Buy some.*) **Vas-y.** (*Go there/Go ahead!*)

Disjunctive Pronouns

The personal pronouns discussed above are conjunctive, that is, they are always joined to a verb either as subject or as object and cannot stand alone. In speech they are never stressed (except in some affirmative commands). Disjunctive pronouns may stand by themselves:

	singular	plural
1st person	**moi**	**nous**
2nd person	**toi**	**vous**
3rd person	**lui** (masculine)	**eux**
	elle (feminine)	**elles**

The conjunctive and disjunctive forms *elle, elles, nous,* and *vous* are the same.

Disjunctives occur:

1. after *c'est* and *ce sont* ("it is"): **C'est moi, c'est toi, c'est lui, c'est elle, c'est nous, c'est vous.** But: **Ce sont eux, ce sont elles. C'est moi qui parle.** (*It is I who am speaking.*) **C'est nous qui l'avons fait.** (*It is we who did it.*) **Ce sont elles qui arrivent.** (*It is they who are coming.*) (In familiar speech only: **C'est eux/c'est elles qui arrivent.**)

2. after a preposition: **Elle parle de lui.** (*She is talking about him.*) **Nous allons avec elle.** (*We're going with her.*) **Je pensais à eux.** (*I was thinking about them.*)

3. after a comparison: **Elle est plus belle qui toi.** (*She is more beautiful than you.*) **Je suis moins jolie qu'elle.** (*I am less pretty than she.*)

4. alone, for emphasis: **Qui est là? Moi.** (*Who is there? I am.*) **Qui regarde-t-elle? Lui.** (*Whom is she looking at? Him.*)

5. to add emphasis to a non-accented pronoun: **Moi, je prépare la salade.** (*Me, I'm making the salad.*) **Et toi, tu fais les sandwichs.** (*And you, you're making the sandwiches.*)

6. after *ne . . . que*: **Elle n'aime que lui.** (*She loves only him.*)

7. as part of a compound subject: **Vous et moi, nous le ferons.** (*You and I will do it.*) **Jean et lui, ils arrivent.** (*Jean and he are arriving.*)

8. as part of a compound object: **Je vous adore, toi et Anne.** (*I love you and Anne.*) **Il nous voit, lui et moi.** (*They see him and me.*)

9. in combination with *même* for emphatic forms (note that *même* agrees with the pronoun it accompanies): **Je le ferai moi-même.** (*I'll do it myself.*) **Ils le trouvent eux-mêmes.** (*They're finding it themselves.*) **Allez-y vous-même.** (*Go there yourself.*) **Cherchez-les vous-mêmes.** (*Look for them yourselves.*)The form *soi* is used with the subject is indefinite: *on, chacun, nul, personne*: **Chacun pour soi.** (*Each one for himself.*)

Possessive Pronouns

A possessive pronoun is used to replace a possessive adjective plus a noun. The possessive pronoun must agree with the noun it replaces and be accompanied by the appropriate definite article or one of its contracted forms (*au, du, aux, des*).

	singular		*plural*	
	masculine	*feminine*	*masculine*	*feminine*
mine	le mien	la mienne	les miens	les miennes
yours (fam.)	le tien	la tienne	les tiens	les tiennes
his, hers, its	le sien	la sienne	les siens	les siennes
ours	le nôtre	la nôtre	les nôtres	les nôtres
your	le vôtre	la vôtre	les vôtres	les vôtres
theirs	le leur	le leur	les leurs	les leurs

J'ai mon livre, non pas le tien. (*I have my book, not yours.*) **Voici tes billets. Et les miens?** (*Here are your tickets. And mine?*) **Je préfère mon livre au sien.** (*I prefer my book to his* [or *hers*]). **J'ai besoin de mes livres. Ont-ils besoin des leurs?** (*I need my books. Do they need theirs?*) **Ils téléphone à leur professeur.** (*They are telephoning their professor.*) **Téléphonons au nôtre.** (*Let's phone ours.*)

Demonstrative Pronouns

French has one form of the demonstrative as the equivalent of English *this one*, *that one*, *these*, and *those*:

	singular	*plural*
masculine	**celui**	**ceux**
feminine	**celle**	**celles**

When followed by a relative pronoun, the demonstrative pronouns mean *the one, the ones, he (she) who, those who*, etc.: **Celui qui entre est mon ami.** (*The one who is coming in is my friend.*)

The demonstrative pronoun followed by *de* indicates possession: **La bicyclette de Pierre et celle de Marie sont bleues.** (*Pierre's and Marie's bicycles are blue.*)

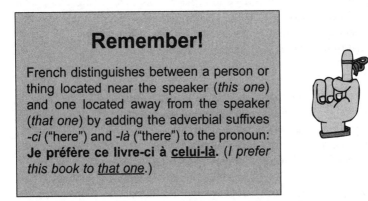

Remember!

French distinguishes between a person or thing located near the speaker (*this one*) and one located away from the speaker (*that one*) by adding the adverbial suffixes *-ci* ("here") and *-là* ("there") to the pronoun: **Je préfère ce livre-ci à celui-là.** (*I prefer this book to that one.*)

When two things are mentioned and referred to again, *-ci* is used to refer to the latter and *-là* to the former: **J'ai rencontré Mme Dupont et M. Leclerc. Celui-ci est homme d'affaire, celle-là est médecin.** (*I ran into Mme Dupont and M. Leclerc. The latter is a businessman and the former is a physician.*)

Ce dernier (*cette dernière*) ("the last") and *le premier* (*la première*) ("the first") may also be used: **Ce dernier est homme d'affaires, la première est médecin.**

Indefinite Demonstrative Pronouns

Ce, ceci, and *Cela (Ça)*

Ce (c') is used with the verb *être*:

1. before a noun that is modified: **Regardez cet homme. C'est un grand pianiste.** (*Look at that man. He's a great pianist.*) **Qui est cette fille? C'est ma sœur.** (*Who is that girl? She's my sister.*)
2. before a proper noun: **Voilà un jeune homme que je connais. C'est André Peirret.** (*There's a young man I know. It's André Peirret.*)
3. before a pronoun: **J'ai trouvé ce paquet. Est-ce le vôtre?** (*I found this package. Is it yours?*)
4. before a superlative: **Voici des cerises. Ce sont les meilleures de la région.** (*Here are some cherries. They are the best in the region.*)
5. before an infinitive: **Le problème c'est de savoir où commencer.** (*The problem is to know where to begin.*)
6. as a neuter subject: **Il est vrai que deux et deux font quatre. Oui, c'est vrai.** (*It is true that two and two are four. Yes, it is true.*) (Note that *ce* is used to represent something that has preceded. *Il* is used to introduce something that follows.)

Ceci, Cela (Ça)

When the demonstrative pronoun replaces an indefinite expression or an idea, *ceci* or *cela* is used. *Ça* is used in familiar style, but never in formal writing. *Cela* is used when the expression has already been mentioned; *ceci* is used to introduce an expression: **Ceci est bon. Vous avez bien réussi.** (*This is good. You have succeeded well.*) **Vous avez réussi. Cela est bon.** (*You have succeeded. That is good.*)

Ceci and *cela* may be used in contrast to mean "the latter" and "the former." **Du cinéma ou du théâtre, ceci me plaît plus que cela.** (*Concerning the cinema or the theater, the latter pleases me more than the former.*)

Relative Pronouns

Qui

Qui functions as the subject of the clause and may refer to a person or to a thing: **La femme qui parle est ma mère.** (*The woman who is speaking is my mother.*)**Le livre qui est sur la table est intéressant.** (*The book that is on the table is interesting.*) **Ce livre, qui m'a beaucoup intéressé, n'est pas bien connu.** (*This book, which interested me a lot, is not well known.*)

In proverb style, *qui* may replace *celui qui*: **Qui aime bien châtie bien.** (*One who loves well punishes well.*)

Qui is also used in certain archaic idiomatic expressions to replace *ce qui*: **Qui plus est, . . .** (*What is more, . . .*) **Qui pis est, . . .** (*What is worse, . . .*) **Qui mieux est, . . .** (*What is better, . . .*)

Que (Qu')

Que functions as the direct object of a clause and may refer to either persons or things. In compound tenses, the past participle agrees in number and gender with the antecedent of *que*. Note that in French *que* may never be dropped: **Les garçons que nous avons vus hier sont mes frères.** (*The boys we saw yesterday are my brothers.*) **Les livres qu'elle a écrits sont bien intéressants.** (*The books she has written are very interesting.*)

Ce qui and Ce que

Ce qui ("what," "that which") is used as the subject of a clause when there is no antecedent: **Comprenez-vous ce qui se passe?** (*Do you understand what is happening?*) **Ce qui est arrivé est presque impossible.** (*What happened is nearly impossible.*)

Ce que ("what," "that which") is used as the object of a verb in a relative clause when there is no antecedent: **Je ne comprends pas ce que vous avez dit.** (*I don't understand what you said.*) **Ce qu'il a écrit est difficile à comprendre.** (*What he wrote is difficult to understand.*)

Ce qui and *ce que* may be combined with *tout* ("everything"): **Tout ce qui est beau est bon.** (*Everything that is beautiful is good.*) **Tout ce qu'elle fait est parfait.** (*Everything she does is perfect.*)

Relative Pronouns with Prepositions Other than *de*

Qui

Qui as object of a preposition refers to persons only: **La fille à qui vous parliez est gentille.** (*The girl with whom you were talking is nice.*) **L'homme pour qui je travaille est intelligent.** (*The man whom I work for is intelligent.*)

Lequel, laquelle, lesquels, lesquelles

Lequel is the relative pronoun used after a preposition, and it refers to things or to persons; it agrees in number and gender with its antecedent. It is identical in form to the interrogative *lequel* (*See* Chap. 6): **La maison dans laquelle Pierre habite est grande.** (*The house in which Pierre lives is large.*) **Le restaurant devant lequel j'ai attendu mon ami est merveilleux.** (*The restaurant in front of which I waited for my friend is wonderful.*) **Les raisons pour lesquelles je fais cela sont évidentes.** (*The reasons for which I am doing that are evident.*)

After *parmi* and *entre*, *lequel* is obligatory and cannot be replaced by *qui*: **Les gens parmi lesquels il vit sont gentils.** (*The people among whom he lives are nice.*) **Les femmes entre lesquelles elle se tient debout sont ses amies.** (*The women between whom she is standing are her friends.*)

Lequel contracts when preceded by *à*. **Le concert auquel il a assisté a été bon.** (*The concert that he attended was good.*) **L'école à laquelle elle va est vieille.** (*The school she goes to is old.*) **Les garçons auxquels nous parlons sont gentils.** (*The boys to whom we are speaking are nice.*) **Les filles auxquelles nous pensons sont gentilles.** (*The girls we are thinking of are nice.*)

Où

A relative clause referring to a place or time is usually introduced by *où* to avoid using a preposition plus a form of *lequel*: **Voilà la maison dans laquelle Georges habite/Voilà la maison où Georges habite.** (*There is the house where George lives.*) **Le siècle pendant lequel il vécut était intéressant/Le siècle où il vécut était intéressant.** (*The century in which he lived was interesting.*)

Relative Pronouns with the Preposition *de: Dont, duquel,* etc.

Dont refers to persons or things and means *whose, of* or *about which, of* or *about whom:* **La femme dont nous parlons est Marie Dupont.** *(The woman about whom we are speaking is Marie Dupont.)* **Le film dont nous parlons est bon.** *(The film we are talking about is good.)* **Je connais une fille dont le père est astronaute.** *(I know a girl whose father is an astronaut.)* **L'homme dont le fils parle est avocat.** *(The man whose son is speaking is a lawyer.)*

> Note the French word order when *dont* refers to the object of the verb: **Voilà un tableau dont j'admire la beauté.** *(There is a painting whose beauty I admire.)* **Voilà le monsieur dont nous avons rencontré la femme hier soir.** *(There is the gentleman whose wife we met last evening.)* **C'est un enfant dont je connais bien les parents.** *(He is a child whose parents I know very well.)*

Dont is used only when it immediately follows the noun to which it refers. If the noun is followed by a prepositional phrase, the appropriate form of *de* plus *lequel* is used: **C'est le garçon avec la sœur duquel je suis sorti.** *(He is the boy whose sister I went out with.)* **Voilà la fille à la mère de laquelle vous avez parlé.** *(There is the girl whose mother you spoke to.)*

Quoi, Ce dont

Quoi is used after a preposition: **Je sais de quoi vous parlez.** *(I know what you are talking about.)* **Je sais à quoi tu penses.** *(I know what you're thinking about.)* **Je sais sur quoi il écrit.** *(I know what he's writing about.)*

Ce dont can be used before expressions requiring *de:* **Ce dont il a besoin, c'est l'argent.** *(What he needs is money.)* **Il sait ce dont tu as envie.** *(He knows what you want.)*

Indefinite Pronouns

1. *l'un (l'une)... l'autre /les uns (les unes)... les autres*: **Voilà deux frères. L'un est riche, l'autre est pauvre.** (*There are two brothers. One is rich, the other is poor.*) **Ce sont de belles femmes. Les unes sont riches, les autres pas.** (*Those are beautiful women. Some are rich, others are not.*) **Elles sont venues l'une et l'autre.** (*Both of them came.*) **Vous avez deux livres. Donnez-moi l'un ou l'autre.** (*You have two books. Give me either one.*) **Ils se détestent l'un l'autre.** (*They hate each other.*) **Ils s'écrivent l'un à l'autre.** (*They write to each other.*) **Elles travaillent l'une pour l'autre.** (*They work for each other.*)
2. *autre chose* (*something else*): **Je voudrais autre chose.** (*I would like something else.*) When *autre chose* is modified by an adjective, the adjective is invariable and it is introduced by *de*: **Je veux autre chose de bon.** (*I want something else good.*)
3. *autrui* (*others, other people*): **Il ne faut pas convoiter le bien d'autrui.** (*You must not covet others' well-being.*)
4. *chacun, chacune* (*each one, everyone*): **Chacun à son goût.** (*Each to his own taste.*) **Chacune des filles apportera un cadeau.** (*Each one of the girls will bring a gift.*)
5. *pas grand-chose* (*not much*): **Il n'a pas grand-chose à me dire.** (*He does not have much to say to me.*)
6. *n'importe qui* (*no matter who, anyone*): **N'importe qui pourra le faire.** (*Anyone can do it.*) **Je parlerai à n'importe qui.** (*I'll talk to anyone.*)
7. *n'importe quoi* (*no matter what, anything*): **Il peut faire n'importe quoi.** (*He can do anything.*)
8. *quelqu'un* (*someone*): **Quelqu'un frappe.** (*Someone's knocking.*)When *quelqu'un* is modified by an adjective, the adjective is invariable and it is introduced by *de*: **Quelqu'un d'important.** (*Someone important.*) **Quelqu'un d'autre.** (*Someone else.*)
9. *quelque chose* (*something*): **Veux-tu quelque chose?** (*Do you want something?*) **Quelque chose ne va pas.** (*Something isn't right.*) When *quelque chose* is modified by an adjective, the adjective is invariable and it is introduced by *de*: **Quelque chose de bon.** (*Something good.*) **Quelque chose d'autre.** (*Something else.*)
10. *quiconque* (*whoever, anyone who*): **Quiconque travaillera mangera.** (*Anyone who works will eat.*)
11. *tout le monde* (*everyone*):**Tout le monde est ici.** (*Everyone is here.*) **Il aime tout le monde.** (*He likes everybody.*)

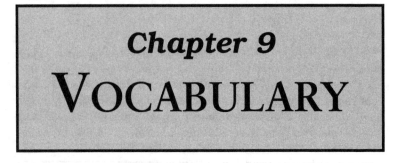

Chapter 9
VOCABULARY

Expressions with *Aller*

Some idiomatic expressions with the verb *aller* are: **aller à la pêche** (*to go fishing*), **aller à la chasse** (*to go hunting*), **aller à pied** (*to go on foot*), **aller à bicyclette, à vélo** (*to go by bicycle*), **aller en voiture, en avion** (*to go by car, by plane*), **aller par le train** (*to go by train*), **aller loin** (*to go far, to succeed*), **aller trop loin** (*to go too far*), **aller bien, mal, mieux** (*to feel, to be well, bad, better*), **aller à quelqu'un** (*to suit, to become someone*): **Elle est intelligente; elle <u>ira loin</u>. Il <u>va trop loin</u>. Je suis très fâché; je <u>vais bien</u> aujourd'hui. Cette robe <u>lui va</u> très bien. Cette robe <u>lui va</u> mal. <u>Allez</u>-y! <u>Vas</u>-y.** (*Go ahead! Do it!*) **Comment allez-vous?/Comment <u>vas</u>-tu?/Comment ça <u>va</u>?** (familiar) (*How are you?*) **Ça <u>va</u>?** (informal) (*How are you?*)

Expressions with *Avoir*

The verb *avoir* is used in many idiomatic expressions: **avoir chaud** (*to be warm, of a person, an animal*), **avoir froid** (*to be cold, of a person, an animal*), **avoir faim** (*to be hungry*), **avoir soif** (*to be thirsty*), **avoir sommeil** (*to be sleepy*), **avoir peur de** (*to be afraid of*), **avoir honte de** (*to be ashamed of*), **avoir raison** (*to be right, of a person*), **avoir tort** (*to be wrong, of a person*), **avoir mal à** (*to have an ache in*), **avoir du mal à** (*to have difficulty [doing something]*), **avoir lieu** (*to take place*), **avoir beau** (*to do something in vain*), **avoir l'air** (*to seem*), **avoir de la chance** (*to be lucky*), **avoir de la patience** (*to be patient*), **avoir . . . de retard** (*to be late by . . .*), **avoir . . . d'avance** (*to be early by . . .*), **avoir envie de** (*to want, to feel like*), **avoir besoin de** (*to need [to]*), **avoir l'habitude de** (*to be in the habit of*), **avoir l'intention de** (*to intend to*),

132

A L'AEROPORT

avoir le temps de (*to have the time to*), **avoir quelque chose** (*to have something wrong*), **avoir . . . ans** (*to be . . . years old*), **avoir à** (*to have to*): Elle <u>a chaud</u> en été. Il <u>a froid</u> en hiver. J'ai <u>très faim</u>; je veux manger. Elle veut de l'eau parce qu'elle <u>a soif</u>. Je vais me coucher parce que j'<u>ai sommeil</u>.Il <u>a peur</u> du lion. Il <u>a honte</u> de ses mauvaises actions.Il pense qu'il <u>a</u> toujours <u>raison</u>, mais cette fois il <u>a tort</u>. J'<u>ai mal à la tête</u> parce que j'<u>ai mal aux dents</u>. Il <u>a du mal à</u> comprendre quand on parle vite. Le concert <u>aura lieu</u> demain. L'action du film <u>a lieu</u> dans une grande ville. Il <u>avait beau</u> étudier; il n'a pas réussi à l'examen. (*It was useless for him to study; he did not pass the exam.*)Elle <u>a l'air</u> contente. Elle <u>a l'air de</u> réfléchir. Marie <u>a de la chance</u>; elle a gagné la loterie. Les mères <u>ont</u> toujours <u>de la patience</u>. L'avion <u>a</u> quinze minutes <u>de retard</u>.Ils <u>ont</u> dix minutes <u>d'avance</u>. Il <u>a envie</u> d'une glace. Il <u>a envie d'</u>aller en chercher. Il <u>a besoin d'</u>eau. Il <u>a besoin de</u> boire un peu d'eau. Il <u>a l'habitude de</u> prendre du thé à quatre heures. J'<u>ai l'intention d'</u>étudier

A BORD DE L'AVION

À LA GARE

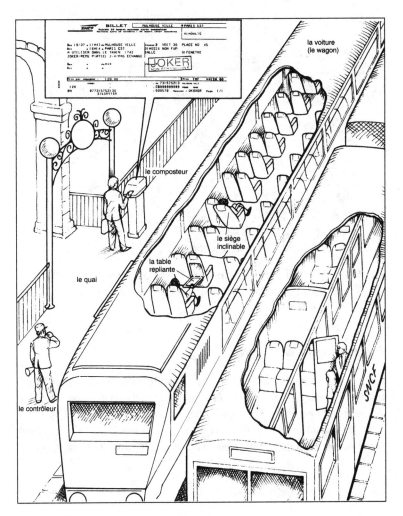

À LA GARE (DE CHEMIN DE FER)

davantage. Je n'<u>ai</u> pas <u>le temps</u> de le faire. Qu'est-ce que vous avez? Vous <u>avez quelque chose</u>? Quel âge <u>avez</u>-vous? J'<u>ai</u> vingt et un <u>ans</u>. J'<u>ai à</u> faire ce travail.

Expressions with *Être*

Expressions with *être* include: **être en train de** (*to be in the act of, in the process of*), **être à** (*to belong to*), **être égal à** (*to make no difference to*), **être de retour** (*to be back*), **Ça y est.** (*That's all right. It's done.*): **Je <u>suis en train de</u> travailler. Cet ordinateur <u>est à moi</u>. Cela <u>m'est égal</u> s'il réussit ou non. Elle <u>sera de retour</u> lundi. Vous avez terminé? Oui, <u>ça y est</u>.**

Expressions with *Faire*

The verb *faire* is used in many expressions relating to the weather: **Il fait chaud.** (*It is warm.*) **Il fait froid.** (*It is cold.*) **Il fait frais.** (*It is cool.*) **Il fait bon.** (*It is nice.*) **Il fait mauvais.** (*It is bad.*) **Il fait beau.**

À LA BANQUE

SUR LA ROUTE

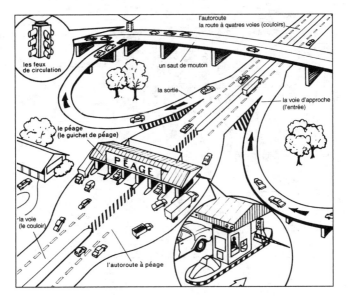

L'AUTOMOBILE

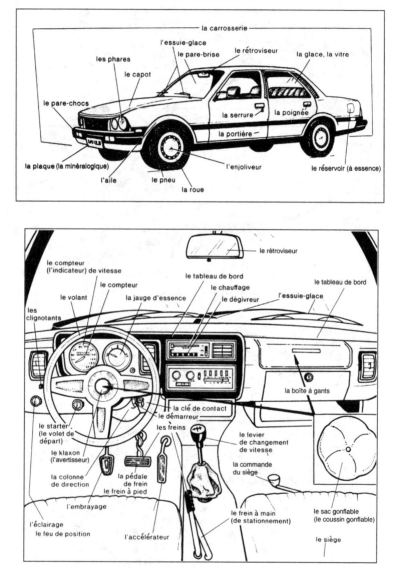

À L'HÔTEL

(*It is beautiful.*) **Il fait du soleil.** (*It is sunny.*) **Il fait du vent.** (*It is windy.*) **Il fait du brouillard.** (*It is foggy.*)

Other expressions having to do with the atmosphere include: **Il fait nuit.** (*It is night.*) **Il fait noir.** (*It is dark.*) **Il fait jour.** (*It is daylight.*)

Other expressions with *faire* include: **faire l'impossible** (*to do the impossible*), **faire de son mieux** (*to do one's best*), **faire de son possible** (*to do the best one can*), **faire du bien** (*to produce a good effect*), **faire fortune** (*to become rich, to be successful*), **faire des économies** (*to economize, to save money*), **faire plaisir** (*to give pleasure*), **faire mal, faire du mal** (*to hurt*), **faire attention (à)** (*to pay attention [to]*), **faire peur à** (*to scare*), **faire la connaissance de** (*to make the acquaintance of*), **faire des courses, ses courses** (*to run errands*), **faire le ménage** (*to do housework*), **faire la queue** (*to wait in line*), **faire un voyage** (*to take a trip*), **faire une promenade** (*to take a walk, a ride*), **faire exprès** (*to do something on purpose*), **faire semblant de** (*to pretend*), **faire des études, ses études** (*to study [at a college or university]*), **Cela (Ça) ne fait rien.** (*It doesn't matter.*): **Des bains de soleil vous <u>feront du bien</u>. Elle s'est <u>fait du mal</u>. Elle s'est <u>fait mal</u> au bras. Il faut <u>faire attention</u>. <u>Faites attention</u> au policier. Je <u>fais attention aux</u> feux rouges. Le tigre <u>leur a fait peur</u>. Hier soir**

À L'HÔTEL

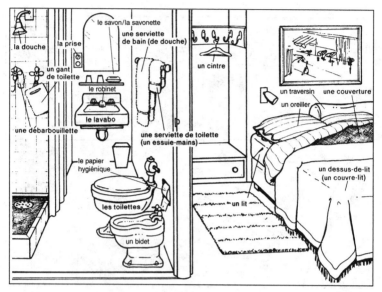

j'ai fait la connaissance de votre sœur. Je faisais mes courses quand j'ai rencontré Hélène. Je t'aiderai à faire le ménage. Nous faisions la queue pendant une heure en attendant le bus. Ils feront un voyage aux Antilles françaises. Le dimanche soir nous faisions une promenade dans le parc. Il a fait exprès de me téléphoner à deux heures du matin. Elle faisait semblant de dormir. J'ai fait mes études à Montréal.

Special Meanings

Devoir, pouvoir, savoir, vouloir

The basic meaning of *devoir* is "to owe": **Je dois cent francs à Jean.** (*I owe Jean a hundred francs.*)

When accompanied by an infinitive, *devoir* implies necessity: **Il doit travailler.** (*He must work.*) **Je devrai partir tôt.** (*I will have to leave early.*)

It may also imply expectation: **Elle doit partir à vingt heures.** (*She is scheduled to leave at 8:00.*) **Il devait arriver à l'heure.** (*He was supposed to arrive on time.*)

À L'HÔTEL

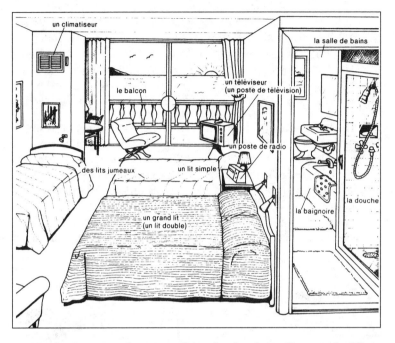

In the present and past conditionals, *devoir* implies moral obligation: **Tu ne devrais pas bouder.** (*You ought not to pout.*) **Ils auraient dû y rester.** (*They should have stayed there.*)

In the present, imperfect, and *passé composé*, *devoir* expresses probability: **Il dort tard; il doit être malade.** (*He's sleeping late; he must be ill.*) **Il a dû rater le train.** (*He must have missed the train.*)

The basic meaning of *pouvoir* is "to be able," "can," "may": **Je peux jouer du violon.** (*I can play the violin.*) **Pourriez-vous m'aider?** (*Could you help me?*) **Vous pouvez vous servir.** (*You may help yourself.*)

In the past, these meanings are conveyed by the imperfect: **Je pouvais travailler tard.** (*I was able to work late.*)

The *passé composé* limits one's ability to a single event; the meaning is most clearly conveyed by "succeeded in": **J'ai pu enfin m'échapper.** (*I could finally escape [=I finally succeeded in escaping]*).

The basic meaning of *savoir* is "to know (a fact)": **Je sais qu'il a trente ans.** (*I know that he is thirty years old.*)

When accompanied by an infinitive, it means "to know how to do something": **Je sais jouer du piano.** (*I know how to play the piano*.)
In the past, these meanings are conveyed by the imperfect: **Je savais qu'il avait raison.** (*I knew he was right.*) **Je savais jouer du piano.** (*I used to know how to play the piano*.)
The *passé composé* limits one's knowing to a single event; the meaning is best conveyed by "found out": **J'ai su alors qu'il avait raison.** (*I knew then that he was right [=I found out that he was right]*).

The basic meaning of **vouloir** is "to want" (something, to do something), "to wish" (to do something): **Je veux la voir.** (*I want to see her.*) **Je voudrais un peu de vin.** (*I would like a little wine.*)
In the past, these meanings are conveyed by the imperfect: **Je voulais la voir.** (*I wished to see her.*) **Je voulais un peu de vin.** (*I wanted a little wine.*)
The *passé composé* limits one's wanting to a single event; the meaning is best conveyed by "tried to" in the affirmative and "refused" in the

À LA PHARMACIE

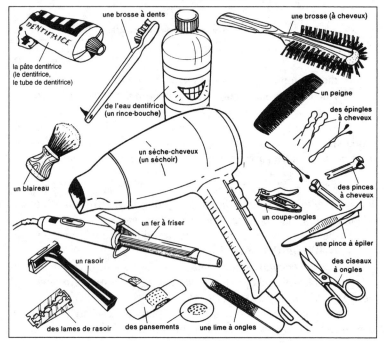

une brosse à dents
une brosse (à cheveux)
la pâte dentifrice (le dentifrice, le tube de dentifrice)
de l'eau dentifrice (un rince-bouche)
un peigne
des épingles à cheveux
un sèche-cheveux (un séchoir)
un blaireau
des pinces à cheveux
un fer à friser
un coupe-ongles
une pince à épiler
un rasoir
des ciseaux à ongles
des lames de rasoir
des pansements
une lime à ongles

A LA POSTE (AU BUREAU DE POSTE)

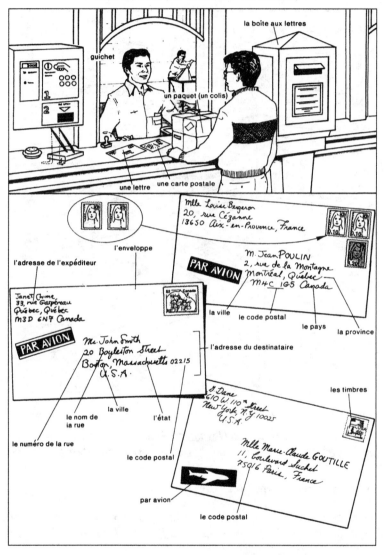

MATÉRIEL ÉLECTRONIQUE

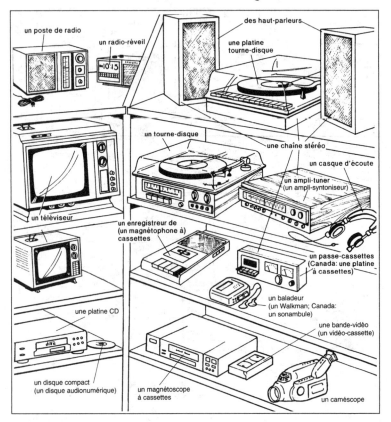

negative: **J'ai voulu la voir.** (*I wanted to see her [=I tried to see her].*)
Je n'ai pas voulu de vin. (*I didn't want any wine [=I refused wine].*)

Habiter, demeurer, vivre (**"to live"**)

Vivre means "to live" in the senses of being alive or, when transitive, of experiencing: **Il vivra longtemps.** (*He'll live a long time.*) **Il vit un cauchemar.** (*He is living a nightmare.*)
    Habiter and *demeurer* mean "to live" in the sense of dwelling in a place: **Il habite à Londres.** (*He lives in London.*) **Il demeure au numéro huit.** (*He lives in no. 8.*)

Habiter is sometimes used without a preposition: **Elle habite Paris.** (*She lives in Paris.*) **Quelle ville habite-t-il?** (*What city does he live in?*)

Jouer

Jouer means "to play" and, when transitive, "to play" a piece of music or a role: **L'enfant joue dans le jardin.** (*The child is playing in the garden.*) **Ils jouent une symphonie.** (*They are playing a symphony.*) **Cet acteur joue le Cid.** *This actor is playing the Cid.*)

The preposition *à* is used before the name of a game: **Si nous jouions au bridge.** (*Let's play bridge.*) **Marc joue au football.** (*Marc plays soccer.*)

The preposition *de* is used before a musical instrument: **Marc joue de la guitare.** (*Marc plays the guitar.*)

Manquer

Manquer means "to miss": **Il a manqué le but.** (*He missed the goal.*) **J'ai manqué mon train.** (*I missed my train.*)

AU BORD DE LA MER

le phare
un bateau à voile (un voilier)
une planche à voile
un bateau à moteur
des skis nautiques
le garde-plage (le sauveteur)
un gilet de sauvetage
un matelas gonflable (pneumatique)
un bateau à rames
une chaise-longue
une chaise pliante
un parasol

LE SALON

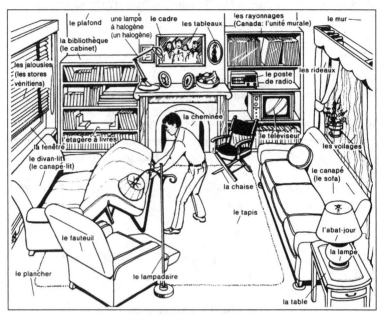

When used with the preposition *à*, it means "to miss" in the sense of feeling sad because someone or something is absent or lacking (note the syntax): **André manque à Marie.** (*Marie misses André.*) **Les cigarettes lui manquent.** (*He misses cigarettes.*)

When used with the preposition *de* followed by a noun, it means "to lack": **Nous manquons d'argent.** (*We are lacking money.*)

When used with *de* followed by an infinitive, it means "to fail": **J'ai manqué de vous le dire.** (*I failed to tell you.*)

Penser

Penser means "to think": **Tu penses trop.** (*You think too much.*)

When used with *de*, it means "to think of," "to think about" in the sense of having an opinion about someone or something (this expression is usually found in a direct or indirect question): **Qu'est-ce que tu penses de Paul?** (*What do you think about Paul?*) **Qu-est-ce que tu penses de lui?** (*What do you think of him?*) **Que pensez-vous de ce**

film? (*What do you* <u>*think about*</u> *this film?*) **Qu'en pensez-vous?** (*What do you* <u>*think about*</u> *it?*) **Il m'a demandé ce que je pense de Paul.** (*He asked me what I* <u>*thought of*</u> *Paul.*) **Il voulait savoir ce que pensais du film.** (*He wanted to know what I* <u>*thought about*</u> *the film.*)

When used with *à*, it means "to think of," "to think about" in the sense of having one's thoughts occupied by a person or a thing: **Je pense souvent à Marie.** (*I often* <u>*think about*</u> *Marie.*) **Je pensais à mes examens.** (*I* <u>*was thinking about*</u> *my exams.*)

Note that when referring to a person, the structure is not that of an indirect object, but a normal prepositional phrase; the noun is replaced by a disjunctive pronoun: **Je pense souvent à elle.** (*I often* <u>*think of her.*</u>) **Il pensait à moi.** (*He* <u>*was thinking about*</u> *me.*)

When referring to a thing, the pronoun *y* is used, as normally, to replace the prepositional phrase: **Je pensais à mes examens.** (*I was thinking about my exams.*) **J'y pensais.** (*I was thinking about them.*)

Partir, sortir, s'en aller, laisser, quitter ("to leave")

Partir is intransitive and, when not used in the absolute sense, is usually accompanied by *de* (the place which one leaves) or *pour* (the place for which one leaves): **Je pars à minuit.** [absolute] (<u>*I'm leaving*</u> *at midnight.*)**Il part de Paris.** (*He's* <u>*leaving from*</u> *Paris.*) **Il part pour Paris.** (*He's* <u>*leaving for*</u> *Paris.*)

Sortir, when used intransitively, means "to go out" (of a place or with someone): **Elle sort souvent.** [absolute] (*She* <u>*goes out*</u> *often.*) **Elle est sort de la maison.** (*She* <u>*left*</u> *the house.*) **Elle sort avec Pascal.** (*She is going out with Pascal.*)

Sortir is used transitively to mean "to take out" (something from a place where it is hidden or put away): **Le voleur a sorti un révolver.** (*The robber* <u>*took out*</u> *a gun.*)

S'en aller means "to go away": **Je m'en vais.** (<u>*I'm leaving. I'm going away.*</u>)**Va-t'en!** (<u>*Get out of here!*</u>)

Laisser is a transitive verb that can mean "to leave" (a person or a thing behind): **Elle y a laissé son livre.** (*She* <u>*left*</u> *her book there.*) **Je laisserai ma sœur au cinéma.** (<u>*I'll leave*</u> *my sister at the movies.*)

Quitter is a transitive verb meaning "to leave" (a place or a person): **Elle quitte la maison.** (*She's leaving the house.*) **Bon soir, je vous quitte**

LA SALLE À MANGER

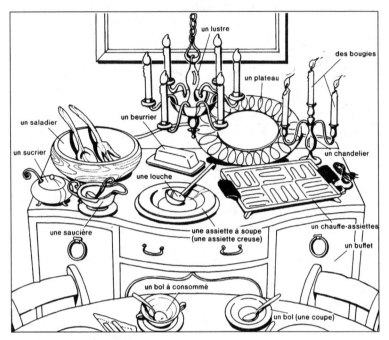

maintenant. (*Good night, I'm leaving you now.*) **Il a quitté** sa
femme.(*He left his wife.*)

Passer

Passer, used transitively, means "to pass" (someone or something
along): **Passe-moi le sel, s'il te plaît.** (*Please pass me the salt.*) **Ne
quittez pas. Je vous le passe.** (*Don't hang up. I'll give him to you.*)

It also means "to go across": **Nous avons passé une rivière.** (*We
went across a river.*) **Ils ont passé la frontière.** (*They crossed the border.*)

Used figuratively in this sense, it means "to take" (an exam): **J'ai
passé un examen de maths.** (*I took a math examination.*)

Used with expressions of time or duration, it means "to spend":
J'ai passé trois jours à Paris. (*I spent three days in Paris.*) **Il a passé
l'été à jouer.** (*He spent the summer playing.*) **Il passe sa vie dans un
rêve.** (*He spends his life in a dream.*)

Used intransitively, it means "to pass," "to go by" (a place): **Je <u>suis</u> passé par la pharmacie.** (*I <u>went</u> by the drug store.*) **Elle <u>est passée</u> chez sa fille.** (*She <u>went by</u> her daughter's.*)

The reflexive expression *se passer de* means "to do without" (someone or something), "to pass up" (something): **Elle <u>se passe</u> très bien <u>d'alcool</u>.** (*She <u>gets along</u> fine <u>without</u> alcohol.*) **Ils <u>se passent</u> <u>d'argent</u>.** (*They <u>are doing without</u> money.*)

Plaire

Plaire ("to please") is often used instead of *aimer* to mean "to like" (the person who is pleased is expressed as the indirect object): **Ce film leur <u>a</u> beaucoup <u>plu</u>.** (*That film <u>pleased</u> them a lot.*)

Se rappeler *and* se souvenir de *("to remember")*

The basic meaning of *se rappeler* is "to recall." Note that in *se rappeler* the reflexive pronoun is an indirect object and the thing or person remembered is the direct object; in *se souvenir de* the reflexive pronoun

AU THÉÂTRE

is a direct object: **Elle s'est rappelé les leçons.** (*She remembered the lessons.*) **Elle se les est rappelées.** (*She remembered them.*) **Ils se sont souvenus des leçons.** (*They remembered the lessons.*) **Ils s'en sont souvenus.** (*They remembered them.*)

Servir and *se servir de*

The basic meaning of *servir* is "to serve": **Elles servent le déjeuner.** (*They are serving lunch.*) **Le vassal sert son seigneur.** (*The vassal serves his lord.*)

The expression *servir à* means "to be used for": **À quoi servent les boucliers?** (*What are shields for?*) **Ils servent à vous protéger.** (*They are used to protect people.*)

The idiom *se servir de* means "to use" (a thing): **Je me sers d'un stylo pour écrire.** (*I use a pen to write with.*)

Savoir versus *connaître* ("to know")

Savoir means specifically "to know" a fact, a reason, how to do something (see above).

Connaître is used with persons, places, works of art, literature, etc. It has the meaning of "to be acquainted with": **Je connais Marie.** (*I know Marie.*) **Il connaît bien le Canada.** (*He knows Canada well.*)

In the past, these meanings are expressed by the imperfect: **Tu connaissais ce poème.** (*You used to know this poem.*) **Je connaissais M. Durand.** (*I knew Monsieur Durand.*)

The *passé composé* of *connaître* limits one's acquaintance to a single event; the meaning is best conveyed by "made the acquaintance of": **J'ai connu M. Durand.** (*I met Monsieur Durand.*)

Index